# Improving the Viability and Perception of HBCUs

# The Africana Experience and Critical Leadership Studies

**Series Editors:**

Abul Pitre, PhD, North Carolina A&T State University
Comfort O. Okpala, PhD, North Carolina A&T State University

Through interdisciplinary scholarship, this book series explores the experiences of people of African descent in the United States and abroad. This series covers a wide range of areas that include but are not limited to the following: history, political science, education, science, health care, sociology, cultural studies, religious studies, psychology, hip-hop, anthropology, literature, and leadership studies. With the addition of leadership studies, this series breaks new ground, as there is a dearth of scholarship in leadership studies as it relates to the Africana experience. The critical leadership studies component of this series allows for interdisciplinary, critical leadership discourse in the Africana experience, offering scholars an outlet to produce new scholarship that is engaging, innovative, and transformative. Scholars across disciplines are invited to submit their manuscripts for review in this timely series, which seeks to provide cutting edge knowledge that can address the societal challenges facing Africana communities.

**Series Titles:**

*Survival of the Historically Black Colleges and Universities: Making It Happen,*
Edited by Edward Fort

*Engaging the Diaspora: Migration and African Families,*
Edited by Pauline Ada Uwakweh, Jerono P. Rotich, and Comfort O. Okpala

*Africana Islamic Studies,*
Edited by James L. Conyers and Abul Pitre

*Improving the Perception and Viability of HBCUs,*
Edited by Kimberly Young Walker and Comfort O. Okpala

# Improving the Viability and Perception of HBCUs

Edited by
Comfort O. Okpala and
Kimberly Young Walker

LEXINGTON BOOKS

*Lanham • Boulder • New York • London*

Published by Lexington Books
An imprint of The Rowman & Littlefield Publishing Group, Inc.
4501 Forbes Boulevard, Suite 200, Lanham, Maryland 20706
www.rowman.com

6 Tinworth Street, London SE11 5AL, United Kingdom

British Library Cataloguing in Publication Information Available

**Library of Congress Cataloging-in-Publication Data Available**

ISBN: 978-1-4985-7864-6 (cloth : alk. paper)
ISBN: 978-1-4985-7865-3 (electronic)

♾™ The paper used in this publication meets the minimum requirements of American
National Standard for Information Sciences—Permanence of Paper for Printed Library
Materials, ANSI/NISO Z39.48-1992.

Printed in the United States of America

# Contents

*Chapter 1*

# An Exemplary Leader in Higher Education

## *A Focus on One Historically Black University*

### Comfort O. Okpala and Kimberly Young Walker

Leadership issues and topics have been discussed and researched for a very long time, and there has been a consistent definition of leadership by a number of researchers as someone with the potential to influence a group of individuals toward the achievement of organizational goals (Greenberg, 2006; Kotter, 1990; Mallo, 1999; Smith, 1961; Yukl, 1998). There are numerous studies on the behaviors and characteristics of leaders from business organizations (Drucker, 1999; Howkins, 2001), but little has been done on leadership characteristics of exemplary academic deans (Wolverton, Amelch, Wolverton, and Sarros, 1999). Most of the studies on academic deans focused on their transition from teaching to academic leadership (Arter, 1981), their skills and mobility (Montez, Wolverton, and Gmelch, 2002), and their level of stress (Gmelch, Wolverton, and Sarros, 1999). This research study is undertaken to add to the body of literature by addressing leadership characteristics of academic deans at one historically Black university. This proposed study is significant in influencing the quality of institutions because as Wolverton et al. (1999) emphasized, about 90 percent of all administrative decisions in higher education are made at the departmental level under the leadership of a dean. Hersey and Blanchard (1982) posit that the study of leadership characteristics is instrumental in the improvement of effective use of human resources.

## LITERATURE REVIEW

The role, behavior, and characteristics of deans vary by institutional and school/college types. Research has shown that the leadership behaviors and characteristics of organizational leaders directly influence actions in the work

1

environment that lead to change (Drucker, 1999; Gilley, 2005; Howkins, 2001). Butler (2007) stated that the work and responsibilities of deans is challenging but rewarding. Bisbee and Miller (2007) emphasized that the duties of deans are more complex in today's environment as they participate in roles like budgets, mediate conflict, address complex personnel issues, attend a plethora of meetings, and endure frequent interruptions. Most deans are selected from senior faculty ranks and as such, serve two roles, that of a scholar and administrator (Gmelch, 2000; Gmelch and Wolverton, 2002; Greenberg, 2006; Reason and Gmelch, 2003). Since deans are responsible for a number of roles and tasks, it is important to examine their characteristics with the use of both task and behavior leadership theories. Gilley (2005) emphasized that institutions of higher education as well as schools and colleges are constantly searching for academic deans with people-centered skills that will use their powers in an ethically responsive way to realize organizational mission and goals.

The purpose of this qualitative case study is to examine and identify the leadership behaviors and characteristics of exemplary academic deans with a focus on African American leaders at a historically Black university in the southeastern United States. The research questions that guided the focus of this study are as follows:

1. What are the leadership behaviors of exemplary academic deans in higher education?
2. What are the perceptions of the participants on the destructive behaviors of academic deans in higher education?

## INTERPRETIVE WORLDVIEW AND
## THEORETICAL FRAMEWORK

John W. Creswell (2009) describes "worldview" as a general orientation about the world and the nature of research that a researcher holds. According to the constructivist/interpretive worldview, researchers acquire knowledge by interpreting the perceptions of their participants (Lincoln, Lynham, and Guba, 2011). Social reality is created and understood through the "construction of knowledge based on the participant's frame of reference within the setting" (Guba and Lincoln, 1985, 80). Denzin and Lincoln (2003) suggest that all researchers are social constructivist and that "knowledge is ideological, political, and permeated with values" (308). Creswell (2009) states that in a constructivist/interpretivist design, researchers look at meanings from the perspectives of informants and tries to understand the experiences based on their relationships. This study is grounded in social constructivist/interpretivist worldview. This paradigm or worldview allows the researchers to gain a deeper understanding by interpreting subject perceptions with authentic representation of data (Denzin and Lincoln, 1998, 106).

The role for organizational leaders, according to Senge (1990), include the ability to build a shared vision, to challenge prevailing mental model, and to foster more systemic patterns of thinking. It is important to state that the researchers in this study have had experiences as leaders and faculty in higher education, so, our interest in this topic rests in our pursuit for academic deans' leadership improvement strategies based on the outcome from this study.

The researchers in this study utilized constructs from Gmelch and Wolverton's (2002) study. The authors posit that for academic deans to become effective, they must perform three activities that include the ability to build a community of scholars, the ability to set direction, and the ability to empower others. These activities also align with the characteristics of transformational leadership. So, this research was grounded within the framework of transformational leadership theory. Transformational leaders utilize a shared vision to inspire subordinates to strive beyond required expectations. Transformational leadership was developed by Burns and elaborated by Bass (Bass, 1990; 1997). The transformational leadership has—as its starting point—the need for the organization to operate smoothly and efficient (Aarons, 2005; Shields, 2011). These authors emphasized that transformational leadership is concerned with achieving organizational change and success within complex and diverse systems. Academic deans are expected to be visionary leaders with roles that are associated with the leadership dimensions described by Heck, Johnsrud, and Rosser in their 2000 study. These dimensions include vision and goal setting; management of academic affairs; developing and maintaining interpersonal relationships with faculty, staff, and students; communication skills; pursuing professional development; research and institutional endeavors; advancing quality of education; and supporting institutional diversity (Heck et al., 2000).

The researcher utilized the High-Performance Organizational (HPO) framework to guide this research in the selection of exemplary deans to interview for the research study. HPO model is about organizations that achieve financial and nonfinancial results and are better than their peer group for over a period of five years or more. Utilizing that framework in an academic environment, academic deans that have served in that role for five years or more and have achieved student and faculty growth were sought in one historically Black university in the South to participate in the study. Only one academic dean met the criteria due to the high turnover rate of the deans in this bounded institution.

## METHODS

A single instrumental case study approach (Yin, 2006) was used to examine and document academic dean's leadership behaviors and characteristics. The case study allowed the researchers to conduct in-depth interviews with few participants. This approach not only illuminated clear knowledge of leadership behaviors of academic deans but also "reformed common sense" (Denzin and Lincoln, 2003, 196), and inform future hiring decisions for academic deans. Case study approach is appropriate for this study because the varying experiences and individual perceptions of the exemplary academic deans are best captured in their own words (Patton, 2002; Walsham, 1990). The researcher utilized HPO framework to select one academic dean who served in that role for forty-two years and has achieved student and faculty growth. This dean as well as selected students, faculty, and staff were the participants for this study.

### Sample

The participants for this study were purposively selected and comprised of fifteen individuals (a dean, three current faculty members, three retired faculty members, three current students, three alumni, and two staff). The dean has served in that role for a number of years and some of the faculty and staff that participated in this study have also served with the dean for a number of years. Two of the retired faculty were hired by the dean in the study. The participants comprised of 60 percent females and 86.7 percent African Americans.

### Data Source and Procedure

Various data sources that include fifteen participants' interview, document analysis, archival records, and observations were used. Johnson and Christensen (2004) posit that the use of multiple perspectives strengthens educational research as it adds insights and understanding that might be missed with a single strategy. The goal of such methodology was to provide stronger evidence for a conclusion through convergence and corroboration of findings (Creswell, 2003; Johnson and Christensen, 2004; Johnson and Onwuegbuzie, 2004; Tashakkori and Teddlie, 1998). Denzi (1978) identified the use of different types of measure as a good methodological triangulation. The researchers sought and received the Institutional Review Board application for the study prior to conducting the study. The participants who were selected for the study were individually interviewed by the researchers using the Academic Deans Leadership Behavior and Characteristics Interview

Protocol. The interviews were conducted in a conference room located on the campus of the institution of the dean in this study. The dean's interview lasted for two hours while the interviews for the other participants lasted for an hour. All the interviews were tape recorded with the permission of the participants. Departmental documents that were available on the websites were examined to document student and faculty growth. Other archival documents and reports were also examined. The participants were also given open-ended questionnaire to freely describe the dean's leadership behaviors and characteristics and to identify destructive behaviors of academic deans in higher education. The data from the survey, interview notes, as well as the tape-recorded data were analyzed.

## Data Analysis

Yin (2006) stated that case study findings are strengthened by a convergence of multiple measures of the same phenomenon. Multiple sources of evidence were used to document the leadership behaviors and characteristics of an academic dean in a historically Black university. Data from the dean, faculty, staff, and students were analyzed. The interview transcripts were transcribed and coded for themes that emerged. The documents and archival records were examined and analyzed. Saldaña's (2006) method of coding was also utilized to sort the themes that emerged for the study. In this approach, the themes were organized based on the frequency of occurrence and the triangulation with other data sources.

## RESULTS

The data from the preliminary analysis vary from the dean to faculty, staff, and students. The results from the dean's data show that the leadership characteristics of exemplary academic deans in higher education stem from the PC (passion and commitment) of academic leadership responsibilities that are embedded in five traits that include character, integrity, trust, excellence, and stability. According to the dean, "An exemplary academic dean must have passion for what the school and the university is all about and must be committed to the development of students, faculty and staff. They must lead with an impeccable character that inspires followers, with strong morals and ethics. That individual must be trusted by all the stakeholders and must lead with a passion for excellence." The dean stated that stability is a mark of commitment to student and faculty growth and development. "There is a difference in the behavior of academic deans in terms of commitment, there are those who are committed to only the position and earnings, those deans will be deans for one day with the aspirations of becoming the provost the next day, and the president or chancellor in three days. Those are the microwave mentality leaders that are never committed to the growth of their department, faculty and students. They are the overly ambitious leaders that will separate from the university in the middle of a semester for another position." The dean emphasized that an institution should never invest in those types of individuals because of the cost associated with turnovers. He continued to state that exemplary deans must have the ability to recruit non-microwave chairs and faculty that will maintain the stability of the department.

The results from the interview data from faculty, staff, and students revealed that the leadership characteristics of exemplary academic deans vary and ranged from building a caring and supportive relationship, passion for excellence, commitment to build a lasting legacy, to courageous politician, and fairness implementer. As one faculty emphasized "an exemplary dean is one that cares about every member of the department and is courageous enough to use a consistent yardstick to assess faculty productivity and merit in a fair and unbiased manner." As one staff participant explained, "a great dean is one that inspires others to yawn for excellence." One retired faculty stated that fairness is the key to faculty happiness. One student stated that when a dean shows that he cares about students' learning and growth, the likelihood that students will perform is greater than lack of concern and caring attitude from the academic deans.

When asked to describe some destructive behaviors of academic deans, the results ranged from lack of passion and commitment, autocratic leadership style, closed-mindedness, to inflexibility. One faculty emphasized that some deans tend to believe that they are the "boss" of the college and forget that they were once faculty as soon as they get into the role of a dean. One retired faculty stated that some academic leaders in higher education tend to be intimidated by other highly competent faculty which leads to "jealous destructive behaviors of iron fist leadership style." "A major destructive behavior for some of the young deans in higher education is their lack of passion and commitment to anything but themselves." It is interesting to note that a majority of the participants cited lack of passion, commitment, and care as the most destructive behaviors of academic deans in higher education.

## CONCLUSION, IMPLICATIONS, AND RECOMMENDATIONS

In this study, the leadership characteristics of academic deans at a historically Black university are examined. One striking observation that emerged from this study was that the dean who participated in this study served in that role for more than forty years and some of the other participants were either students or faculty and staff under his deanship. The findings from the study show that strong passion and commitment to the growth and development of students, faculty, and staff are important leadership characteristics of academic deans in higher education as well as stability in the position. The findings from this study have policy and practical implications. Due to the high turnover rates in the position of deans at the university in this bounded instrumental case study, it is critical to implement university-wide hiring policy that will focus on hiring and developing academic deans that will maintain the stability of the school or college. In this era of accountability and budget cuts with increased demands to retain students, the role of an exemplary academic dean has never been more important than now.

This case study yielded triangulated results on the leadership characteristics and destructive behaviors of academic deans in higher education. Due to the low sample size from this study, it is recommended that further studies be carried out with more participants for stronger results. It is also recommended that the use of mixed-method approach may yield stronger results. Since this case study was bounded in one public university, it is recommended that multiple sites that will include both public and private universities and colleges be utilized for further studies.

## BIBLIOGRAPHY

Bess, J., and Wally, S. (2003). Strategic decision speed and firm performance. *Strategic Management Journal*, 24(11), 1107–1129.

Butler, J. (2007). *The essential academic dean: A practical guide to college leadership.* San Francisco, CA: Jossey Bass.

Creswell, J. (2009). *Research design: Qualitative, quantitative and mixed methods approaches* (2nd ed.). Thousand Oaks, CA: Sage Publications.

Denzin, N. (1978). *The research act: A theoretical introduction to sociological methods.* New York: McGraw-Hills.

Denzin, N., and Lincoln, Y. (2003). *The landscape of qualitative research: Theories and issues* (2nd ed.). Thousand Oaks, CA: Sage.

Drucker, P. (1999). *Management challenges for the 21st century.* New York: HarperCollins.

Gilley, A. (2005). *The manager as a change leader.* Westport, CT: Praeger.

Gmelch, W., Wolverton, M., Wolverton, M. L., and Sarros, J. (1999). The academic dean: An imperial species searching for balance. *Research in Higher Education*, 40(5), 717–740.

Greenberg, M. (2006). The power of academic citizenship. *The Chronicles of Higher Education*, 52(22), B29.

Guba, E., and Lincoln, Y. (1994). "Competing paradigms in qualitative research." In N. Denzin and Y. Lincoln (Eds.), *SAGE handbook of qualitative research* (105–117). Tousand Oaks, CA: SAGE.

Hersey, P., and Blanchard, K. (1982). *Management of organizational behavior: Utilizing human resources* (4th ed.). Englewood Cliffs, NJ: Prentice-Hall.

Howkins, J. (2001). *The creative economy*. London: Penguin Books.

Johnson, B., and Christenson, L. (2004). *Educational research: Quantitative, qualitative, mixed approaches* (2nd ed.). Boston, MA: Pearson Education Inc.

Kotter, J. (1990). *A force for change: How leadership challenge differs from management*. New York, NY: The Free Press.

Montez, J., Wolverton, M., and Gmelch, H. (2002). The roles and challenges of dean. *Review of Higher Education, 26*(2), 241–266.

Patton, M. (2002). *Qualitative evaluation and research methods* (3rd ed.). Thousand Oaks, CA: Sage Publications.

Shields, C. M. (2010). Transformative leadership: Working for equity in diverse contexts. *Educational Administration Quarterly, 46*(4), 558–589. doi: 10.1177/0013161x10375609.

Wolverton, M., Gmelch, W., Wolverton, M. L., and Sarros, J. (1999). Stress in academic leadership: US and Australian department chairs/heads. *The Review of Higher Education, 22*(2), 165–185.

Wolverton, M., Wolverton, M. L., and Gmelch, W. (1999). The impact of role conflict and ambiguity on academic deans. *Journal of Higher Education, 70*(2), 80–106.

Yukl, G. (1998). *Leadership in organizations* (4th ed.). Upper Saddle River, NJ: Prentice-Hall.

*Chapter 2*

# The Leadership behind the Leader

## *Examining Boards of HBCUs and the Potential Effect That These Members Are Having on HBCUs Success and/or Failure*

### Terrance M. McAdoo

A recent article written by Dr. Walter Kimbrough, president at Dillard University, revealed an alarming and sad revelation regarding the instability of the presidency/chancellor position at many historically Black colleges and universities (HBCUs). Dr. Kimbrough wrote that, on average, HBCU presidents, over the last 7 years, only remained at their respective institutions for approximately 3.3 years before leaving that particular institution (Kimbrough, 2017). This means that presidents/chancellors rarely stay beyond the initial contract which is typically three years. This is particularly bothersome because several HBCUs have closed in recent years, and if the president's position continues to turn over at such an alarming rate it's easy to predict that others will close as well. In fact, one former HBCU chancellor predicts just that. Former HBCU chancellor (North Carolina A&T State University) Dr. Edward B. Fort has suggested that the right individuals are not being chosen to lead these institutions and, as a result, the revolving door of the HBCU president/chancellor continues. His book *Survival of the Historically Black Colleges and Universities: Making It Happen* outlines significant factors for success and reasons for failure of HBCUs. This chapter looks to examine further the work of Dr. Kimbrough, Dr. Fort, and others and extend their research to more closely examine the boards, who, in most cases, select these presidents/chancellors of HBCUs.

## WHAT ARE BOARDS OF TRUSTEES, AND WHY DO THEY EXIST?

Before diving into the demographic information in regard to the boards of trustees who were examined in this study, the author thought that it would be beneficial to discuss why boards of trustees are needed and how they are often selected. Corporations often have board of directors whereas institutions of higher education normally have boards of trustees, boards of regents, and boards of governors. According to the Association of Governing Boards of Universities and Colleges (www.abg.org, 2017), "boards of trustees," "boards of regents," and "boards of governors" are terms used with organizations that are typically in the not-for-profit arena, which, in most cases, includes institutions of higher education (note: there are a several for-profit institutions of higher education in the United States and they have board of trustees). Whether boards of directors or boards of trustees (or regents/governors), there are researchers who believe having a board is vital to the sustainability and growth of an organization. Patel (2015) declared that there are at least five reasons that boards are needed, which include skills and expertise of board members, (institutional) corporate governance, independence and accountability, strategic direction, and credibility and legitimacy.

Skills and expertise is necessary for institutions because leaders are not great at everything, thus board members may often provide expertise in one or several areas needed for the institution that cannot be provided by the president or chancellor. Patel (2015) states that "Board of Directors will help the senior leadership to step back from the daily operational grind and focus on its business." Governance help is vital because board members can assist in setting the rules, systems, common practices, policies, and procedures of the organization. Independence and accountability are important because board members typically act without fear of some sort of business conflict and they hold the CEO, president, or chancellor accountable for the success or failure of the vision, mission, and goals of the institution. The board should help organizations' strategic direction in several ways: (1) It should hold the leader accountable for the direction of the organization, while also (2) contributing to that direction via engagement in aligning the institution with future outcomes that will benefit the institution, and (3) board member's strategic direction, along with leadership, help set a time frame for which these future action should occur. Lastly, in regard to creditability and legitimacy, Patel (2015) stated, "an effective board portrays integrity, and availability of balanced objective advice which help mitigate risk."

Boards of trustees are often selected by state political leaders or parties that are tied to the governing and funding of the university. For example, Tuskegee University's board is comprised of twenty-five voting members, five of which are appointed by the governor of Alabama, and the others are state appointed members. The appointment of board of trustee members by the governor or state appointment is a common practice. For example, South Carolina State University's board of trustee members are appointed by the General Assembly of South Carolina. North Carolina's public Universities are also similarly structured. Eight of thirteen board of trustee members at institutions such as North Carolina A&T State University and Winston Salem State University (eight of thirteen also) are identified and selected by the University of North Carolina (UNC) Board of Governors and four are selected by the Governor of North Carolina. The UNC Board of Governors is controlled and selected by the General Assembly of North Carolina. The UNC Policy Manual, which was created by the North Carolina General Assembly, describes the aforementioned establishment and structure of the UNC Board of Governors. It is particularly important to examine the structure of boards of trustees in the state of North Carolina because North Carolina has the most HBCUs within its borders. In fact, two of the ten HBCUs that were examined in this study reside in the state of North Carolina. The point of discussing the selection/construction of boards and board members is to provide insight into how board members come into power, and how one's state political system, influence and climate can have a significant impact on who becomes a board member.

## FLAWS IN BOARD'S LEADERSHIP SELECTION

Are HBCU boards of trustees bad at selecting good leaders? The answer to this question is relative, and depends on multiple variables linked to how we assess the success or failure of these leaders. Is a good leader one who stays over seven years and accomplishes little? It is doubtful. But, if taxpayers, the African American community, the academy, and others interested in the vitality of HBCUs are using time dedicated to the position as the baseline for measuring leaders' success, then what Dr. Kimbrough has identified as problematic is indeed a lack of success. Certainly, it is possible that some leaders can generate positive change in a limited period of time, but it is also likely that any strategic plan developed and implemented has yet to be fulfilled in the short three-year time span that many presidents/chancellors spend at HBCUs before departing. Kimbrough's (2017) article points to Dr. Stephen Trachtenberg's book on the derailing of college presidents, in which Dr. Trachtenberg, President of George Washington University, stated that a college president who does not extend into a second contract is a failed presidency. This is understandable because new leadership often signifies new direction, new goals, and new agendas. This type of change, on a consistent basis, can leave an institution unfocused and unidentifiable. As with all products and services, or more specifically companies and organizations, an institution must have a unique niche and target market. Constant changes in direction and goals of the institution can muddle that niche until what was once a strength of the university or college is now unrecognizable. The vetting process performed by board members may need to change. Cohn and Moran (2011) suggest measuring seven unique attributes when selecting a leader: integrity, empathy, emotional intelligence, vision, judgment, courage, and passion. They believe that these attributes are paramount to a leader's success and are built into the fabric of an effective leader, almost like DNA. Burns (1978) points to the concept of moral leadership which ties into the integrity attribute that Cohn and Moran mentioned. Are boards of trustees examining the integrity of the candidate and their history regarding moral and ethical decision-making? Does the president/chancellor candidate have a propensity for leaving for higher compensation before adequately implementing his or her agenda and/or goals set during his or her time as the leader at the former institution? Does the candidate show a genuine interest in the needs and well-being of the followers before and after he or she exits an institution? Is the lure of urban life so great that presidents and chancellors at rural HBCUs are doomed to keep their leader in place even when the leader does not exhibit high levels of integrity and morality? All of these questions are things HBCU board members should consider during the presidential/chancellor search process.

## ALARMING TRENDS OF HBCU PRESIDENTS/CHANCELLORS

Kimbrough (2017) provides a solid starting point regarding the recent trends of HBCU presidents/chancellors and their exit from an array of historically Black colleges and universities over the last fifteen plus years. He stated, "For the past decade, I have kept a running log of HBCU presidential transitions . . . a widely known fact—there is a lot of turnover at the top of HBCUs. Between 2010 and 2016, there have been an average of 11 new presidents each year for the 78 four year HBCUs, with the high point being 15 in 2015." This alarming trend has to be disturbing to board members of HBCUs all over the country, unless the instability of these institutions is the goal of the board. What is also troublesome is the lack of gender diversity at the presidential level. Kimbrough also stated that women remained in position as president/chancellor at a similar pace as men, yet they only represent approximately 30 percent of all HBCU presidents. Many of these are trends that are a direct result of board of trustees' decisions regarding the leaders' selected. After learning of the impact (i.e., the high turnover) of these decisions, the researcher thought it would be beneficial to examine the make-up of the ten largest HBCUs and their boards of trustees. Methods used to collect this data are in the "Methodology" section of this chapter.

## METHODOLOGY

Data collected on the colleges examined in this study was derived from research via each school's website and the *US News & World*'s report on "Best Colleges." The 2017 *US News & World Report*'s "Best Colleges" was used to ascertain the population size of each institution, in addition to any population data on each school's website. If the population data was easily accessible on the schools' website, that information was used in substitution for the US World New Report-Best Colleges regarding the population of that institution. Additionally, any website hyperlinks provided by the institutions was used to examine that school's governing body (i.e., board of governors, board of trustees, or board of regents) was used to assist in the collection of demographic and other information used in this study.

Board of trustee members who are currently serving terms during the Fall 2017 semester were included in this study. The board member's name, former or current occupation(s), gender, and race/ethnic background were collected. The race/ethnic background data was based solely on picture images posted by the University or College, and thus, cannot be stated as 100 percent accurate in regard to the person's exact race or ethnicity. The data collected was entered into a spreadsheet where it could be disaggregated and analyzed easily.

### Data Analysis

As indicated, the researcher chose the ten largest historically Black colleges and universities in the United States. These included Southern University, North Carolina Central University, Morgan State University, Prairie View A&M University, Tennessee State University, Texas Southern University, Jackson State University, Florida A&M University, North Carolina A&T State University, and Howard University.

There were 128 total number of board of trustee members from the 10 schools studied. This number excludes Student Body (SGA) representatives on boards. Of the 128 members, 96 or 75 percent of them were men, of this, 46.5 percent were either business owners or executive-level business personnel with a significant number of trustee members in the banking industry, 13.2 percent were attorneys. This means that approximately 60 percent of all board members in the top ten largest HBCUs are either businesspersons or attorneys. Educators, which included some attorneys and businessmen/businesswomen who served in the classroom, made up 16.4 percent. Former or current politicians made up 7 percent. Medical doctors made up approximately 8.5 percent. Ministers and ex-military individuals made up a small percentage of trustees at 4.6 percent and 3.1 percent, respectively.

Other data points collected included race/ethnicity, those that were former judges, high-level federal government administrators, and former college presidents/chancellors. The exact race/ethnicity of those who are not Black or African American was not collected. Of the 128 board of trustee members in this study, 101 or 78.9 percent appeared to be Black, African American, or of African descent. There were 3 or 2.3 percent ex-judges, 5 or 3.9 percent high-level federal administrators, and only 3 or 2.3 percent former college presidents/chancellors.

## Discussion

What does this data mean? There is a multitude of educated assumptions that could be derived from the aforementioned board of trustee data. However, what cannot be disputed is that African American/Black men make up the vast majority of the decision makers in the boardroom. Additionally, as Dr. Kimbrough pointed out, African American/Black men make up the vast majority of the individuals that occupy the president/chancellor space. Therefore, it is quite logical to assume that African American men who occupy these spaces will play a critical role in fixing this short-term presidential/chancellor problem, if it can be fixed. Part of that solution may mean that African American/Black men must be willing to reconstruct boundaries and provide a more welcoming environment for women to come in and assist in attempting to bring stability to the presidential/chancellor office at these institutions. Although Kimbrough's research stated that women who occupy or have occupied the president/chancellor space remained in office approximately the same amount of time as men, the author of this chapter believes that more diverse boards can play a role in changing how long women are retained. The change in the traditional "men's club" environment to a more inclusive one might create an atmosphere more conducive to female leadership. This is not to say that having women at the helm of these institutions or having a more equitable share of women at the board table will by itself fix the problem, however, it appears that heterogeneity may bring a new voice, a non-masculine approach and/or alternative thoughts in the room, which may sustain and promote these institutions. Those who have worked in education and/or have researched education of PK–12 and higher education institution know that women make up the vast majority of the faculty and staff. Maybe women leaders of faculty and staff, because they share the same gender and in many cases share the same struggles in a masculine society can garner a more shared leadership outlook. This conceptualization of women in leadership is becoming more prevalent and has made substantial gains in the last thirty years, but overall it is still atypical and thus warrants further scrutiny by board of trustees looking to stabilize the president/chancellor position.

## Discussion: HBCU Boards Unlike other Boards

The peculiarity of the make-up of boards in higher education is that they are mostly made up of individuals who are not educators or have never been educators. The research in this chapter clearly shows that our politicians (general assembly) lean heavily toward selecting businessmen and businesswomen to oversee the leaders of HBCU institutions. This appears to be counterintuitive and unlike other coveted boards, such as boards with Certified Public Accountants (CPA) and boards with lawyers (American Bar Association [ABA]). According to the Virginia Board of Accountancy and North Carolina Board of CPAs, all members, except public at-large members, must be certified public accountants to serve on CPA boards (Virginia Board of Accountancy and North Carolina Board of Certified Public Accountants, 2018). The ABA board of governors is similarly comprised of mostly persons from their profession, that is, lawyers (Americanbar.org, 2018).

Maybe the businessmen and businesswomen of HBCU boards are great at identifying CEOs of business companies because that's their background but are not as astute at identifying educational leaders and thus need more training in this regard. This doesn't mean that business professionals cannot contribute valuable input toward selecting leaders and enhancing the viability of HBCU institutions, however, what is being suggested is that individuals with educational background/experiences should have more representation on boards of trustees at HBCU.

Certainly, all or even most of the blame cannot be placed solely on the business people who serve on HBCUs boards. Other professions represented must also bear some of the responsibility, and what must be imperative for all board members is their focus on the vitality, viability, and stability of these institutions. Gassman (2017), a two-time HBCU board member, stated, "board member must ask themselves why they are serving, and if the reason is not connected to the welfare of students, and the overall benefit of the institution, they must resign." Gassman (2017) stated this in light of the troubles at Morehouse college regarding a board chairperson's power and the undercutting of the president of the institution. It is easy to see that an environment such as this could lead to a president resigning quick (in the 3.3 years' window) and moving on to another job.

## WORDS FROM A FORMER HBCU CHANCELLOR: 11 THINGS A PRESIDENT MUST DO OR HAVE FOR SUCCESS

A review of literature aids in the understanding of the current HBCU presidential/chancellor dilemma, however, speaking with a person who has sat at the helm of one of these institutions is invaluable. The author of this chapter was able to conduct an interview with Dr. Edward B. Fort, chancellor emeritus at North Carolina Agricultural and Technical State University. Not only has Chancellor Fort been at the helm of an HBCU, but also he was chancellor at a majority institution, and superintendent at two school districts as well. This allows him to speak knowledgeably about these types of challenges at various types of institutions.

In the interview, Chancellor Fort gave the following insights regarding the reasons for presidential/chancellor success and/or failure and why he believes presidential/chancellor turnover has been a problem. Chancellor Fort stated:

*Interview question: What are the keys to being a successful president, what should board members look for?*

Boards should become more and more familiar with the necessary aggressiveness that I am going to outline:

1) The board has to know how to manage the issue of the chancellorship/presidential selection process driven by the number 1 priority, which is, can the person maintain and grow fiscal accountability at the institution. They have to pick someone who can hire the right people, particularly the Vice President or Vice Chancellor for fiscal affairs, who knows internal and external procedures particularly as they relate to audits. [Presidents/Chancellors] can't get around the idea of someone who has a handle on fiscal accountability. That handle can be enhanced, not necessarily by a PhD or EdD, but by someone who possesses a CPA or MBA. The gentleman that I hired to handle it, to be Vice Chancellor of fiscal affairs, came after the institution [NC A&T] had gone through 4 people in 5 years at that position. Boards have the responsibility for ensuring the fact that the person selected as president has the experience and knowledge base, the two of them, with regard to fiscal management. This person has to have a sound understanding or expertise in fiscal management and can liaison effectively with federal, state and regional fiscal authorities and has the capability of hiring a budget director who has some experience on a post-secondary education basis as far as the management of fiscal affairs and even more so possesses a CPA, MBA, or both. The gentleman I hired, McIntyre, had both.

Additionally, this fiscal accountability issue has to be one where the Deans are held accountable for onsite fiscal management accountability at their domain at their schools, at their colleges, and the chancellor or president has a system in place or can put one in place that can ensure that kind of fiscal management by the deans. That is achieved by having a comprehensive developed staff procedure.

2) Relates increasingly to the issue of enrollment management. The board must ensure that the person hired has the knowledge base or can get the person who can deal effectively and aggressively with enrollment management. In terms of organization accountability, the person should report directly to the provost or the chancellor. This person hired for enrollment management has to

be able to projection enrollment trend one month out, a semester out, three years out. Additionally, this person must be conversant with marketing techniques and K–12 liaison. And on that basis, the enrollment management person has to be at least at the middle management of the hierarchical structural level. He or she has to have the capability of creating a comprehensively developed liaison relationship with K–12 constabularies. That means that the K–12 connectivity is critical in the relationship toward ensuring that the presence of that university on that campus is forever, it's noticeable, and it's attractive in relationship to the ability to advertise what goes on at the university.

3) The critically important task of hiring a chief of staff who has expertise in branding, marketing and knows the ins and outs of the university. That person must have the complete confidence of the chancellor.

4) The [incoming chancellor/president] has to have an acute understanding of and the ability to deal with foundation and corporate relations. It does not matter whether it's a public institution or private. The relationship must be one where he or she hires a staff that not only has knowledgeable contacts with key personnel in foundation and in the corporate sector but knows how to use those in conjunction with particularly the procurement of grants, equipment and providing for on-site staff development and faculty at that institution. Also, the board has to raise some very acute questions including: how are you going about cultivating foundations? And what are you doing about [new jobs created and/or new companies located] companies in your location. How will your faculty/staff aggressively make sure the presences of the university is a known fact when companies like apple come to your area.

5) Curriculum Development. That curriculum development enhancement should at the very least become increasingly focused on offering STEM related courses and programs up and down the line. And that STEM relationship has all kinds of possibilities in terms of dollars earmarked for that university depending on the competencies of not just the chancellor or president but those that he or she hires to deal with the whole issue of . . . well it's the Vice Chancellorship of Curriculum or Provost. That means taking a look at umm I'll just mention two, increasing the presence of baccalaureate programs, graduate and PhD programs, and how are you going to get the money to fund them. That was a question asked of me when I first became chancellor. When I began this full court press to bring in the first PhDs, the first question faculty asked was how are you going to pay for it. And that gets into not only one's proclivity with regard to one's relationship with the state, but also how good are you in relationship to federal funding and the funding that comes from the corporate section and foundations. And so on that basis, one fact knowing full well that one of the degrees that we were going for was electrical engineering and industrial engineering. We knew we had to have money for that. So, to start this thing off we got a umm $400,000 startup grant from the Department of Energy that was placed in the hopper with regard to being used by the PhD program in electrical engineering. So, the person [Chancellor or President] has to have the ability to know the waterfront concerning curricular advancement, starting with STEM.

6) The board must expect that this new CEO or Chancellor/President is going to be able to ensure organizational integrity. And I mean organizational integrity that's job one, first rate, no questions asked.

*Interview question: how can they ascertain that from an interview?*

They are going to have to not only interview that candidate but also go to the campus where that person is and talk to people who have worked with the candidate and raise the issue of integrity because it's not just a mom and pop expectation it's a survival expectation for the university. And if the integrity is not there then take a look at Bowman and Deal's book or Peter Northouse's book on leadership. It addresses ensuring the organization's integrity. And then . . . there has to be a sense that the integrity permeates the institution, no one is just looking the other way, there's no chance for Enron, everyone in on the watch.

7) Accreditation. That has hindered a number of institutions, both public and private. And so the board is going to have to have proof of the fact that the person being hired is one who can handle the challenge of the accreditation process, and knows how to hire persons that have a strong knowledge in this area. Bring one or two of them in as consultant and give them the opportunity to train faculty and staff. So, the whole issue of the handling the accreditation game is something that has wounded Black campuses many of or some of which are private. In that regard then this person will have to zero in on the weaknesses that are inherent in the curriculum, zero in on the weaknesses that relate to the maintenance of fiscal integrity, zero in on the enrollment, and find out, what's the real reason why enrollment is so low. And so, on that basis there again, you've got to hire an experienced consultant one with a knowledge on accreditation, and then expose faculty and staff of his or her knowledge.

8) There will probably have to be a dramatic curtaining of some expenses, and the boards' responsibility is to see if the would-be president has the guts to do so. Some of these cuts will be dramatic. At the same time, they will have to be interface with the cuts that are being promulgated by the state government and the institution that is impacted. That's a tall order. Because it gets at this whole issue of cuts. And course cuts have impacted many HBCUs in this country. So, the whole issue of the impact of state legislative cuts on the institution, be able to deal with it. Be able to deal with it aggressively.

9) The next thing that boards must insist with regard to the incoming president or chancellor is can they conduct a full court press regarding on the adequacy on federal agency liaison. And if the initial overview shows that there is not much going on there or that there could be a lot better than it is then you're going to have to do it to go for it. My suggestion would be not necessarily a concentration on . . . but an aggressive funding move on federal agencies such as the department of energy, department of health and human services, the labor department, this helps with dollars to assist school with their HR program and believe or not dollars with construction. The department of education is a must in relationship to lobbying. Last, particularly if you're a land grant institution,

you cannot separate yourself from the secretary of agriculture and the history of the 1890s that's a part of that secretary.

10) Next, is the issue of achievement and students, you're going to have to increase, for some it's at-risk, the number of young people who come in with high SAT and high honor averages 3.50 or higher. And with that kind of a track record you, can probably increase the support that you get from corporate and foundations.

11) Lastly, [the aforementioned] are not meant to be inclusionary, but just a sample of my life and my experiences as chancellor. It is the issue of pursuing a path that enables the university to have increasingly notable degrees thus globalizing campus and you began to bring in faculty and students from all over the world.

These 10 or 11 points are irrevocably inevitable if one is to survive and grow stronger.

*Interview question: Dr. Fort after looking at these 11 things that you've highlighted, do you think candidates don't have these things in mind when they take the job or are boards not aware that a candidate needs great knowledge of all of these to be successful? Is this the reason for the high turnover?*

I think it's probably two things:

1) The challenge is unexpectedly tough. And umm . . . the individual hired just simply doesn't have the fortitude to endure the pain while strategizing and more, to turn the organization around. The university presidency, particularly of a Black campus, is probably the toughest job in education with the exception of possibly the superintendent. I know that because I've done both. Once in Michigan for five years and once in California for three. These are tough jobs. It takes someone maintaining focus 24/7. It's constant, it's ongoing, and it's about relationships. It's about cultivating relationships. It's about bridging the gap between oneself and those around you. Because if you don't have the loyalty of your faculty and staff you can forget it.

2) The other reason for this rapid turnover is that some boards in their desire to enhance that institution are just not satisfied with what that person is doing. They may say to themselves that we can do better. Sometimes they can, sometimes they can't. And so the only they can find out is by not renewing that contract or if it's that bad just out right releasing that person.

*Interview question: What do you believe are some other factors?*

Well, unfortunately, there are those who take these jobs only for personal gain. They are not concern with the well-being of institution. That individual really need not apply.

*Interview question: Do you believe that the lack of diversity within these boards (because I have found that 75 percent are men and a large percentage are businesspeople) is a contributing factor in the selections of short-term presidents?*

Interesting that you've found that. I would be curious to learn more about that. With regard to business people being involved, it's likely because they are more interested in what kind of contribution can they make to ensure the talent needed for their businesses will continue to be available to them.

The bottom line is that the challenges are massive, but they are not insurmountable. If I had believed that I would not have come to North Carolina A&T State University.

*Interview question: Did you know that you were going to stay 18 years as chancellor of A&T?*

Yes, my wife and I came to A&T with the goal, if everything worked out, of staying for 15 years.

## THE MEANING: FINAL THOUGHTS

Chancellor Fort's comments and insight in conjunction with the author's research regarding HBCUs board of trustees should give those interested a deeper insight into reasons for high presidential turnover, presidential failures, and/or presidential success. What should be clear after reading the aforementioned is that HBCUs viability and existence, as institutions of higher education, can flourish or die at the hands of good or poor leadership. Both board of trustees and presidential/chancellor leaders who take these presidential/chancellor jobs are in position to affect African American life. It is the author's hope that both groups recognize their long-term impact and approach their responsibility with the proper reverence.

## BIBLIOGRAPHY

American Bar Association. (January 10, 2018). Retrieved from https://www.americanbar.org/ groups/leadership/ board_of_governors.html.

Cohn, J., and Moran, J. (2011). *Why Are We Bad at Picking Good Leaders? A Better Way to Evaluate Leadership Potential.* Hobokon, NJ: John Wiley & Sons.

Fort, E. (2013). *Survival of Historically Black Colleges and Universities: Making it Happen.* Lanham, MD: Rowman & Littlefield, Lexington Books.

Gasman, M. (March 28, 2017). At Morehouse: When College Board of Trustees Won't Let Presidents do their Jobs. https://www.washingtonpost.com/news/grade-point/wp/2017/03/28/at-morehouse-when-college-boards-of-trustees-wont-let-presidents-do-their-jobs/?utm_term=.359dd4428615.

Is a board of trustee the same as a board of regents? What is a board of governs? (November 17, 2017). https://www.agb.org/faq/is-a-board-of-trustees-the-same-as-a-board-of-regents-what-is-a-board-of-governors.

Kimbrough, W. (2017). Trends of the HBCU Presidency Demand Attention. https://hbcudigest.com/trends-of-the-hbcu-presidency-demand-attention.

North Carolina State Board of Certified Public Accountant Examiners. (January 9, 2018). https://nccpaboard.gov/about/#heading-2.

Patel, Y. (2015). 5 Reasons Why Every Company Needs a Board of Directors. https://www.linkedin.com/pulse/5-reasons-why-every-company-needs-board-directors-yazad-patel/.

UNC Policy Manual. (December 8, 2017). http://www.northcarolina.edu/apps/policy/index.php?pg=dl&id=4406&format=pdf&inline=1.

U.S. World News Report-Best College. (December 10, 2017). https://www.usnews.com/best-colleges/rankings/hbcu.

Virginia Board of Accountancy. (January 10, 2018). http://www.boa.virginia.gov/Home/board-members.shtml.

*Chapter 3*

# The Making of a HBCU President

## *A Case for Transformational Leadership in Challenging Times*

### Jesse Ford and Rosline Sumpter

Presidents of historically Black colleges and universities (HBCUs) work to educate a population of students who seek an affordable, accessible, and quality postsecondary education. Historically Black colleges and universities serve to celebrate Black culture and history, develop Black leaders, and improve the Black communities that they surround (Allen et al., 2007). In many ways, HBCUs and their presidents have paralleled the history of Black Americans after the Civil War through historical, economic, political, and cultural changes (Allen et al., 2007; LeMelle, 2002; Willie et al., 2005).

Because of the racial, political, and economic hardships that some HBCUs face, a narrative of HBCUs being in crisis is often perpetuated (Medina and Allen, 2017; Rivard, 2014; Schexnider, 2017). However, HBCUs are faced with emerging concerns such as enrollment decline, continual failure to meet performance funding metrics, faculty and presidential turnover, and institutional funding. Although these issues are common for many other postsecondary institutions, they are often exacerbated at HBCUs. For this reason, transformational leadership at HBCUs is crucial to help these institutions maintain their place in the current educational landscape. Transformational leadership requires leaders to transcend their own interests for the sake of others (Northouse, 2013). Presidents of HBCUs must look to the history of their establishments and use it as a guide for transformation and innovation.

Therefore, the purpose of this chapter is to examine how HBCU presidents can lead and affect change in institutions that are rich in history and student success but hindered by various internal and external influences. Specifically, this chapter presents a guiding framework for HBCU transformational leadership. It is posited that transformational leadership is needed to guide HBCUs through challenging times and the current educational landscape.

To help HBCU presidents lead these organizations, a transformational leadership and change model is presented.

## HISTORICAL CONTEXT

### Origins

Before the framework is presented, it is important to understand and revisit
the origins of HBCUs and their historical context. The mission of the first
HBCUs was to educate the select few who were free Blacks before the Civil
War. In 1837, Richard Humphrey founded "The Institute for Colored Youth
(Cheyney University)," the first historically Black college in Philadelphia,
Pennsylvania (Allen et al., 2007). Prior to the Thirteenth Amendment and
before the Civil War, the United States had only nine historically Black colleges primarily because the majority of enslaved Black Americans were not
allowed to learn how to read and write. After gaining freedom, many Black
Americans viewed education as the great equalizer and educational institutions started to form throughout the nation (Allen et al., 2007; LeMelle, 2002).

Between 1861 and 1870, seven Black colleges and thirteen normal teaching
institutes were established (Allen et al., 2007; Cantey et al., 2013; LeMelle,
2002). Most of the early HBCUs were found, led, and developed by churches
and local community organizations. The presidents of these institutions were
often selected, governed, and policed by the churches and local organizations
that founded them (Allen et al., 2007). In order to maintain good financial
standing, many HBCU presidents turned to northern White missionaries and
philanthropists. The donors of funding for many of these institutions often
influenced the president's decisions on curriculum, educational goals, and
graduation requirements (Abelman, 2009; Allen et al., 2007). The roles of
presidents in this era centered on their ability to fundraise, provide direction
over faculty, and maintain strong relationships with donors (Abelman, 2009).

The federal government also established several HBCUs in the mid- to late
1800s. In 1862, the federal government signed the First Morrill Act (Allen et al.,
2007; Cantey et al., 2013; LeMelle, 2002). This Act was signed to establish
educational institutions in states throughout the United States. However,
due to racial tension and discrimination, seventeen states excluded Black
Americans from studying at these land-grant institutions. As a result, the second Morrill Act of 1890 created land-grant colleges for Black students who
were being excluded from institutions established by the Morrill Act of 1862
(Allen et al., 2007; Bettez and Suggs, 2012; Cantey et al., 2013).

The mission of these institutions was to provide a place for underrepresented populations to obtain an education and today, this is still a core

mission of these institutions. By the year 1900, over hundred higher educa-tion institutions were created to educate Black Americans and these institu-tions educated some of America's most prominent Black leaders, including Booker T. Washington, Martin Luther King Jr., Ralph David Abernathy, Langston Hughes and modern leaders Jesse Jackson, Thurgood Marshall, and Herman Cain (Brown, 2010). The curriculum that Black American leaders learned would impact the educational system of these institutions for years to come.

At HBCUs, the role of college presidents looks different than at predomi-nantly White institutions (PWIs). Former president of Tuskegee Institute (Tuskegee University), Booker T. Washington once said, "the individual who can do something that the world wants done will, in the end, make his way regardless of his race" (Cantey et al., 2013, 4). The quote stated by Wash-ington in the 1800s was used to express a turn of the century problem in the United States (Allen et al., 2007; Willie et al., 2005). The Civil War ended in 1865 and a period of reconstruction took place in the United States. Educa-tion, healthcare, and jobs became topics of discussion for these newly freed people (Allen et al., 2007; Willie et al., 2005). Many, including American activist and leader, W. E. B. Du Bois, believed that education would be the foundation of establishing Black Americans in the United States post–Civil War. He stated, "education must not simply teach work—it must teach life" (Brown, 2010).

Early curriculum designs at many of the original HBCUs focused on vocational and industrial training, but as time went on, more liberal arts insti-tutions appeared (Allen et al., 2007). The leadership of institutes similar to Hampton and Tuskegee shaped student learning to focus on elementary edu-cation, manual work, and societal rules (Cantey et al., 2013; Harper, Patton, and Wooden, 2009). Booker T. Washington, president of Tuskegee, served as a leader within the world of education for many early presidents. Many early HBCU presidents mirrored his style, which followed a vocational/industrial model of educating Black Americans. His vision was to "increase the moral-ity of Black students, mitigate conflict between the races and foster White middle-class values" (Harper et al., 2009). He viewed education as a way to teach Black Americans practical skills that would increase their moral-ity, self-reliance, and their economic advancement. Due to his vision, many colleges and institutes opened their doors to all students. Historically Black colleges and universities not only enrolled students ready to be educated at a college level, but also enrolled students who needed secondary educational needs (Allen et al., 2007; Brown, 2010; Cantey et al., 2013; Harper et al., 2009; LeMelle, 2002).

Despite President Washington's views on a vocational education, politi-cal leader W. E. B. Du Bois opposed him. Du Bois strongly disagreed with

President Washington's views and expressed the need for Black colleges to teach more of a liberal arts education (Allen et al., 2007; Brown, 2010; Cantey et al., 2013). At the time, both vocational and liberal arts HBCUs allowed Black Americans to serve as teachers, campus leaders, presidents and administrators which were opportunities they could not receive at predominately White institutions.

## The Impact of the 1954 Decision
## and 1964 Legislation through the 1990s

Inequalities such as a lack of funding and poor infrastructure affected the development of HBCUs during this time period. Despite these challenges, before 1954, 90 percent of all Black students were educated at HBCUs (Allen et al., 2007; Cantey et al., 2013). In 1954, the US Supreme court ruled in the *Brown vs. Board of Education, Topeka, Kansas* case that "separate, but equal," which was established by *Plessy vs. Ferguson* in 1896, was unconstitutional. *Brown vs. Board of Education* paved the way for additional educational programs, opportunities, and jobs for Black Americans. By the time *Brown vs. Board of Education* was passed, many HBCUs presidents, governing boards, funding, curriculum, and functions were shaped by White educators and scholars (Allen et al., 2007; Bettez and Suggs, 2012; Cantey et al., 2013; Crawford, 2017; LeMelle, 2002).

Following *Brown vs. Board of Education*, the Civil Rights Act of 1964 was also passed in the United States. The Civil Rights Act of 1964 officially recognized 114 HBCUs. Congress defined a historically Black college and university as any college or university established before 1964, whose primary mission was to educate Black Americans (Allen et al., 2007; Crawford, 2017; Esters and Strayhorn, 2013). The purpose was to provide public funds to desegregate higher education systems. The Act also made it illegal for colleges and universities to discriminate against students based on race, color, or nationality. In addition, this fueled what higher education scholars call the "Great Migration," which is used to represent the influx of students from HBCUs to historically White institutions (Cantey et al., 2013; Esters and Strayhorn, 2013). This period caused many HBCUs to face a level of identity threat. By desegregating PWIs, Black students had more options to attain education and subsequently made HBCUs appear as a secondary option.

These two major federal acts would change the climate and landscape of HBCUs and their presidents. Historically White institutions started recruiting high achieving Black students, leaving their HBCU counterparts to enroll students who were not as academically prepared (Esters and Strayhorn, 2013). This change would also cause a shift from college-level instruction to remedial education for many of these institutions. During the 1980s and 1990s scholarship funding trends shifted as high achieving students received more funding from PWIs, which resulted in these HBCUs, receiving less funding (Bettez and Suggs, 2012; LeMelle, 2002). During this period, presidents needed to be knowledgeable of fundraising, administrative needs, planning, and communicate with internal and external constituents.

## The Current Status of HBCUs and their Presidents

In 2015, there were 102 HBCUs, accounting for approximately 2 percent of all institutions of higher education in the United States (National Center for Education Statistics, 2018). Of these 102 institutions, 41 are public 4-year institutions, 10 are public two-year institutions, 50 are private 4-year institutions, and 1 is a private 2-year institution (College Navigator, 2018). Out of the 50 states, 19 are home to HBCUs. The following states are home to 6 or more HBCUs: Alabama, North Carolina, Georgia, Texas, South Carolina, Mississippi, Tennessee, and Louisiana (National Center for Education Statistics, 2018). In addition, the District of Columbia is home to 2 HBCUs and the US Virgin Islands is home to 1 HBCU.

Currently, 14 percent of all Black undergraduate students attain degrees from HBCUs (National Center for Education Statistics, 2016). During the 2014–2015 academic year, HBCUs conferred 4,627 associate degrees, 33,413 bachelor's degrees, and 9,917 graduate degrees (National Center for Education Statistics, 2016). Total HBCU enrollment for the Fall 2015 semester was 293,316 students with Black students accounting for 78 percent of the total enrollment.

In a study focused on the background characteristics of HBCU presidents, Freeman and Gasman (2014) found that 16 percent of all HBCU presidents have held their position between 10 and 25 years, 42 percent held their position between 5 and 9 years, and 42 percent held their position between 1 and 4 years. Over half of the HBCU presidents (i.e., 53 percent) were between 60 and 70 years old. While 30 percent of the presidents were female, this finding indicated that little progress has been made in female leadership over the past 30 years. However, the percentage of female HBCU presidents remains higher than the percentage of female presidents at postsecondary institutions overall.

Freeman and Gasman's (2014) study also examined the educational backgrounds of HBCU presidents. In all, 58 percent of HBCU presidents held PhDs, 25 percent held EdDs, 14 percent held JDs, and 3 percent held MDs. An important finding was that 75 percent of HBCU presidents held degrees in education, which is substantially higher than the general population of postsecondary presidents. Additional results indicated 46 percent of HBCU presidents were presidents prior to holding their current presidency and 33 percent of the presidents were either a provost or vice president of academic affairs. An issue that was highlighted in the study was the percentage of presidents who have served in a long-term capacity. Freeman and Gasman (2014) indicate that long-term presidencies can be problematic due to the reliance on the president in unhealthy ways and the risk of hindering new ideas and progress.

## TRANSFORMATIONAL LEADERSHIP

The termination, resignation, and exit of college presidents over the past few years have sparked concerns over the state of HBCUs (e.g., Kimbrough, 2014). Issues of ethical decision-making, leading practices, limited resources, and campus financial difficulties have impacted the way these institutions function and the way presidents lead and make changes within them. In addition to these issues, the role of media outlets has also shaped the perception of how these organizations are managed and led.

According to Brown (2010), a HBCU college president's ability to promote the best image of students, promote and train effective leaders, fundraising for the organization, and reduce levels of negative publicity are important to the future development and survival of these institutions. In the early years of American higher education, university presidents were said to be extraordinary, heroic, and charismatic leaders of institutions who served as community and public leaders (Hefner, 2014; Thelin, 2004). Today, the role of a college president is less involved in public and community engagement efforts and more invested in maintaining relationships with trustees, lawmakers, students, faculty, alumni, fundraisers, media outlets, private businesses, and donors (Hefner, 2014). The need to be a more transformative leader is becoming increasingly important, especially at HBCUs.

Northouse (2013) describes transformational leadership as a process that changes and transforms people and is concerned with emotions, values, ethics, standards, and long-term goals. Transformational leadership incorporates charisma and visionary leadership in an effort to influence and move followers to accomplish more than what is usually expected of them. Additionally, Bass (1998) describes transformational leaders as inspirational, intellectually stimulating and/or individually considerate. Attention to the needs and motives of followers and helping followers reach their full potential are key attributes of transformational leaders. It is important to note that transformational leaders are concerned with the collective good and transcend their own interests for the sake of others (Northouse, 2013).

Bass (1998) describes transformational leadership as an expansion of transactional leadership. Transactional leadership emphasizes the transaction or exchange between leaders and followers. However, transformational leadership goes beyond exchanges to achieve superior results. Specifically, there are four factors that are attributed to transformational leadership: (1) idealized influence, (2) inspirational motivation, (3) intellectual stimulation, and (4) individualized consideration (Bass, 1998; Northouse, 2013). Idealized influence, or charisma, describes leaders who serve as role models for followers and have high standards of moral and ethical conduct. Inspirational motivation describes leaders who behave in ways that motivate and inspire those around them by providing meaning and challenge to their followers' work. Intellectual stimulation describes leaders who stimulate their followers' efforts to be innovative and creative by questioning assumptions, reframing problems, and approaching old situations in new ways. Individualized consideration describes leaders who pay special attention to each individual follower's needs for achievement and growth by acting as coach or mentor.

## A GUIDING FRAMEWORK: TRANSFORMATIONAL LEADERSHIP AND CHANGE

As HBCU presidents face new challenges and changes, they must be flexible and able to garner support from key stakeholders. For this reason, transformational leadership is arguably most effective. In addition to the need for leaders to be transformational, they also must be able to change institutions to better serve their target populations. Bass and Dee (2012) define change as the alteration in the processes, structures, and behaviors within a system. Specifically, transformational changes are needed within HBCUs. A transformational change also provides a major renovation for organizational structures and strategies (Bass and Dee, 2012).

A review of the extant literature found several correlations for skills needed for a president to successfully lead an institution: board management, collaboration, cultural/historical traditions, vision, communication, fundraising, entrepreneurial disposition, and the ability to understand and negotiate with faculty (Bettez and Suggs, 2012; Esters et al., 2016; Freeman and Gasman, 2014; Freeman et al., 2016; Harper et al., 2009; Willie et al., 2006). For years, HBCUs have faced challenges of leadership, student preparedness for college-level work, and financial resources. In addition, the successful recruitment, retention, and development of HBCU presidents has been increasingly challenging over the past fifty years (Abelman and Dalessandro, 2009). Figure 3.1 posits a HBCU transformational leadership and change model. This model incorporates transformational leadership for key areas of concern for HBCUs. Each component of the model is discussed in detail (see figure 3.1).

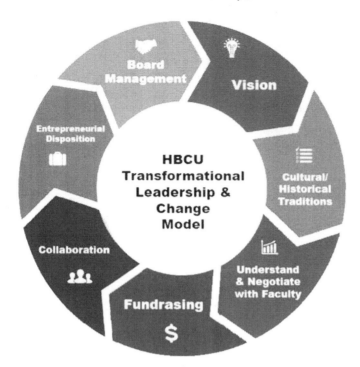

**Figure 3.1 HBCU Transformational Leadership and Change Model.** This figure outlines the seven areas that need to be addressed by HBCU presidents to affect transformational change in the organization.

## Vision

In simple terms, vision is defined as the ability to anticipate and plan for what is to come. The current postsecondary landscape requires leaders to be adept in various areas. This is especially true for HBCU leaders. For example, HBCU presidents must be tuned in to what is happening locally, statewide, and nationally. Changes in political leadership can bring policy and funding changes.

Freeman et al. (2016) utilized the Leadership Pipeline Model developed by HBCUs to examine the role of vision in leading these organizations. The findings revealed the importance of a president to not only think strategically, but also shift their thoughts to thinking globally. One president in the study stated,

> I think that leading an HBCU is redeeming, transformative and you need to be able to communicate to a larger audience that HBCUs are important. Early HBCU presidents saw their mission as being beyond just serving a population of young men and women who came in the door, they were going to become change agents and be able to transform. (Freeman et al., 2016, 4)

This president saw his work as being transformative and necessary to lead his organization.

In addition, HBCU presidents need to be innovative, entrepreneurial, leaders in the African American community, and be able to listen to others for input. These aspects imply a transformational component. Transformational vision includes getting other people to see what the future holds and helping the institution to prepare for it. Without vision, HBCUs will lack direction, which would subsequently hinder their success. Vision is a key component in the role of being a transformational leader, change maker, and president.

## Communication

A HBCU president must be able to communicate effectively with a diverse group of people. Advocating for resources, support, and funding are concerns that must be discussed with policy makers, donors, and campus entities. Communication is a key component to any leadership position. However, the ability to make communication transformative is key for HBCU leadership.

Making communication transformative incorporates the factors of transformational leadership, that is, idealized influence, inspirational motivation, intellectual stimulation, and individualized consideration. Presidents of HBCUs must be able to communicate their enthusiasm to help motivate and stimulate others. It is also important that listening is a key component of the communication process. Transformational leaders talk, but also listen, since followers and their buy-in are the key distinguishing features in transformational leadership.

Furthermore, it is essential that presidents navigating external environments, such as political constituents, and internal environments, such as faculty and students, be able to cater their message to the appropriate audience. Participants in the Freeman et al. (2016) study identified that a HBCU president must be transparent, flexible, versatile, and accessible and be able to interact with various groups and stakeholders. Great communication can help guide institutions through times of crises and other challenges.

## Fundraising

College presidents have spent more time fundraising than ever before. For the past twenty-five years, fundraising has been a vital part of the college presidential role (Brown, 2010). Since their founding, for many HBCUs, fundraising has been an important part of their survival. Grants, scholarships, veteran benefits, federal loans, and student fees are not stable funds, but have been increasingly important to the success of the institutions (Williams, 2016). The ability to connect with alumni, external partners, and other university partners to expand fundraising efforts has become essential.

Furthermore, fundraising often manifests itself differently in the HBCU community (Gasman, Lundy-Wagner, Ransom, and Bowman, 2010). For this reason, a transformative way of conducting fundraising is needed for HBCUs. As previously mentioned, transformative leaders have a unique way of influencing others. For HBCU presidents, the key stakeholders in fundraising opportunities are alumni. If HBCU presidents can gain buy-in from alumni, it can translate into giving. Engagement from alumni could also help with seeking sources from other stakeholders.

Finally, it is important that HBCU presidents realize their limitations in this area. While HBCU presidents are the face of the organization, it is important to hire the appropriate personnel to help the transformative leader put their vision into place. Development officers and the infrastructure to support development activities are important. Additionally, ongoing training and technical assistance are also important in fundraising at HBCUs (Gasman, Lundy-Wagner, Ransom, and Bowman, 2010).

## Entrepreneurial Disposition

HBCUs hold a unique place in American history. For this reason, it is important that HBCU presidents realize this uniqueness and pursue an entrepreneurial disposition. An entrepreneurial disposition involves a blend of risk-taking, innovation, vision, and strategy. Additionally, HBCUs presidents must think about the postsecondary niche that their institutions hold and use that to their advantage.

In recent years, state governments have explored ways to trim budgets and eliminate the duplication of services. Many government officials are suggesting HBCUs be consolidated or eliminated to save state funds. In 2011, the Louisiana State Legislature recommended that Southern University (a HBCU) and the University of New Orleans (a PWI) merge to form the University of Louisiana at New Orleans. The merger did not receive the votes needed for the institutions to form the newly consolidated university, but it reinforces the need for HBCU presidents to have entrepreneurial dispositions (Albritton, 2012). In 2015, the state of Georgia consolidated Albany State University with non-HBCU Darton State College. The new institution will preserve the Albany State University name and HBCU mission.

Mergers for HBCUs can pose an array of issues for Black Americans. The cultural, traditional, and historic legacy of these institutions could be lost due to the threat on their identities. Bess and Dee (2012) state that identity threat is external condition that rapidly and dramatically affects the identity of the organization. An entrepreneurial disposition, combined with transformational leadership, can help prevent the loss of identities during challenging times. Entrepreneurs must always find ways to be innovative and often take on greater risk. The same approach must be taken with HBCUs in order to maintain their place in the postsecondary landscape.

## The Ability to Understand and Negotiate with Faculty

Understanding the importance of shared governance, faculty, and academic freedom are critical to the role of HBCU presidents. Many HBCUs face difficulty in attracting and retaining PhD-level faculty members (Cantey et al., 2011). Issues of supporting and retaining faculty are often affected by the quality of students, institutional support, and accreditation of the college or university (Brown, 2011; Cantey et al., 2011; Gasman et al., 2013). To be successful, HBCU presidents must engage and support faculty. The intellectual resources that faculty bring to a campus enhance the mission of the institution. Additionally, student success is often tied to the faculty who educate them.

Understanding and negotiating with faculty requires a level of charisma and influence, key components in transformational leadership. For the institution to succeed, HBCU presidents must incorporate faculty needs into their vision. To help provide the best educational opportunities for students, faculty must be motivated and dedicated to the development of students. Moreover, the presidents of HBCUs must show support and value their faculty members. Additionally, HBCU presidents must be transformative in their ways of recruiting and retaining faculty. Well-known faculty with strong teaching and research records can increase enrollment and funding for the institution.

## Board Management

The ability to work effectively with an institution's governing board is critical to the success of a president. Transformational leadership can make the relationship between governing boards easier to navigate if executed appropriately. Understanding the people on the board is also important to how these relationships are formed and maintained (Gasman, 2010). Furthermore, the ability to be able adapt to changes within the board are important for the success of HBCU presidents. For a leader to be transformational, the support of the board is needed, and no president will be able to lead or affect change without it (Hefner, 2014).

Additionally, the recruitment of board members can vary by state and institutional type. Board members can have different roles within the local community or organization. Presidents of HBCUs must have the ability to recognize the diversity among board members. Recognition of this diversity is important in understanding their expectations and using that knowledge to make transformative change. To make changes within the organization, a relationship between the president and the board will lead to effective decision-making and changes for the survival of the institution.

## Collaboration

Transformational leadership thrives through collaboration. The ability to listen, provide feedback, and consult with others is important in being a collaborative leader. As a collaborative leader, a HBCU president must be willing to listen and learn from others. Additionally, the need to be able to provide clarity for internal and external constituents about roles, responsibilities, and expectations are needed to lead these institutions. As one president reported,

> You have to be a collaborative leader. People want to be consulted. They want their voice heard. You have to consider other people's notions about what's right and what direction the university should follow. If you don't do this, the institution is going to perceive that you are jamming an agenda down their throats without conferring appropriately. (Freeman et al., 2016, 9)

HBCU presidents must strengthen their programs and partnerships with other higher education institutions. For example, several universities have created joint programs to strengthen their academic fields, including Florida Agricultural and Mechanical University and Florida State University (College of Engineering), University of North Carolina at Greensboro and North Carolina A&T State University (Master of Social Work Program and School of Nano-science and Nano-engineering) (Albritton, 2012). These programs show the importance of collaboration within organizations and how important they are for the survival of these institutions. An important collaboration that four-year HBCU presidents should look to strengthen is partnerships with community and technical colleges. Community colleges can provide a pipeline of students who are looking to obtain their bachelor's degree after completing an associate degree. Transfer and articulation agreements with these institutions can provide opportunities for both institutions to thrive.

## Respect for Historic Culture and Traditions within the Community

Historically Black colleges and universities' connections to the community have dated back to the founding of these institutions. Leaders of HBCUs must be dedicated to serving underrepresented students, populations, and communities. Within the communities where HBCUs are located, their presidents have always been viewed as leaders (Brown, 2010). The ability to uplift and empower these local communities is part of the mission of these institutions. In addition, the ability to respect institutional traditions while being innovative are skills that HBCU presidents must adapt to a transformational leadership style. These skills are tied directly to the leadership of HBCU presidents and their ability to respect the traditional, cultural and historical legacy of these institutions and make changes that respect the culture and traditions of these institutions.

## CONCLUSION

Historically Black colleges and universities are "people's universities." They were built for the people, are rich in history, and will stand the tests of time. However, HBCU presidents must be transformational in their leadership and governing of these institutions. Today, many HBCUs play a critical role in filling the educational and workforce needs of their communities. These institutions provide opportunities to populations of students who may not have the opportunity to access higher education.

This chapter has presented a framework for HBCU leaders to reference as they employ the skills needed to become transformational leaders. Transformational leadership requires innovation, risk-taking, understanding, communication, and the transcendence of one's own interests for the sake of others. As current HBCU presidents and board members look to identify the future talent of the organization, it is important that they recognize these types of qualities in individuals.

Furthermore, it is important that researchers seek opportunities to study HBCU leadership in the current educational landscape. The dearth of current literature on HBCUs, particularly leadership, should be a call to action. Additionally, HBCUs should be open to these researchers and grant access. The successes and challenges of HBCUs should be studied to help move these institutions forward. Finally, the diversity among HBCUs must be acknowledged. Private HBCUs operate differently than public HBCUs and four-year HBCUs have different missions than two-year HBCUs. Further research should explore the differences among HBCUs and how leadership varies within this sector. As our world continues to evolve, we need to know what works, how it works, and what we can do to develop HBCU presidents of the future.

### Practical Example—Case Study

Smallville College is a public, Southern HBCU located in a rural, low-income area of the state. In the past five years, the college has experienced a 20 percent enrollment decline and currently has a total enrollment of 1,100 students. Historically, the college has served as an integral part of the community and educates many individuals from the surrounding areas. In recent years, the college has had a successful basketball program and recruits many out-of-state athletes. Popular programs at the college include its undergraduate STEM programs and master's programs in history, public administration, and business administration. Annually, the college attracts alumni from all over the country to its homecoming events increasing the income of the city by 20 percent over one weekend. There are several alumni chapters across the United States, which are also very active in the recruitment, fundraising, and support of the institution.

Last year, the college's state governing body received several complaints about the college's administration. An investigation by state and federal officials found issues with the mismanagement of funds. The president and several executive-level leaders resigned or were fired. The investigation also found that members of the college's board of trustees were interfering in the day-to-day operations of the college and personnel matters. Because of this investigation, several faculty and staff members have left the college. The faculty and staff who remain are uncertain of their future at the college and overall morale at the college is deflated.

You have been appointed to interim president of the college in the middle of the spring semester. There are several faculty and staff who have also been appointed to interim positions due to departures. Several key positions at the college, including vice president of student affairs, financial aid director, and grants coordinator, are vacant.

1. Describe how you would approach this situation with regard to the faculty and staff, students, and board of trustees.
2. Who are the key stakeholders that you would engage while serving as interim president?
3. What elements of transformational leadership would you employ to improve the college for the upcoming school year?
4. What would be your six-month plan to improve the morale of the staff members who stayed at the institution?
5. As an interim president, how would you use specific, measurable, achievable, relevant, and time-bound (SMART) goals to improve conditions at the institution? What would be your goal?

## BIBLIOGRAPHY

Abelman, R., and Dalessandro, A. (2009). The institutional vision of historically Black colleges and universities. *Journal of Black Studies, 40*(2), 105–134.

Albritton, T. J. (2012). Educating our own: The historical legacy of HBCUs and their relevance for educating a new generation of leaders. *Urban Review: Issues and Ideas in Public Education, 44*(3), 311–331.

Allen, W., Jewell, J., Griffin, K., and Wolf, D. (2007). Historically Black colleges and universities: Honoring the past, engaging the present, touching the future. *The Journal of Negro Education, 76*(3), 263–280.

Avolio, B. J., and Bass, B. M. (2004). *Multifactor leadership questionnaire* (Third Edition). Mind Garden Inc.

Bass, B. M. (1998). *Transformational leadership: Industry, military, and educational impact.* Mahwah, NJ: Lawrence Erlbaum Associates.

Bess, J. L., and Dee, J. R. (2012). *Understanding college and university organization: Theories for effective policy and practice* (2 Vols.). Sterling, VA: Stylus.

Bettez, S. C., and Sugg, V. L. (Eds.). (2012). Centering the educational and social significance of HBCUs: A focus on the educational journeys and thoughts of African American scholars. *The Urban Review, 44*(3), 303–310.

Brown, E. D. (2010). *Four-year historically Black college and university president: An examination of leadership styles, values, and attributes.* ProQuest Dissertations Publishing.

Cantey, N., Bland, R., Mack, L., and Joy-Davis, D. (2013). Historically Black colleges and universities: Sustaining a culture of excellence in the twenty-first century. *Journal of African American Studies, 17*(2), 142–153.

Crawford, J. (2017). HBCUs: Accreditation, governance and survival challenges in an ever-increasing competition for funding and students. *Journal of Research Initiatives, 2*(3), 1–12.

College Navigator. (2017). *College navigator: Historically Black colleges and universities.* https://nces.ed.gov/COLLEGENAVIGATOR.

Commodore, F., Freeman, S., Gasman, M., and Carter, C. M. (2016). "How it's done": The role of mentoring and advice in preparing the next generation of historically Black college and university presidents. *Education Sciences, 6*(14), 1–14.

Esters, L. L., and Strayhorn, T. L. (2013). Demystifying the contributions of public land-grant historically Black colleges and universities: Voices of HBCU presidents. *Negro Educational Review, 64*(1), 119–135.

Esters, L., Washington, A., Gasman, M., Commodore, F., and O'Neal, B. (2016). *Effective leadership: A toolkit for the 21st century historical Black college and university president.* Philadelphia, PA: University of Pennsylvania, Center of Minority Serving Institutions.

Freeman, S., and Gasman, M. (2014). The characteristics of historically Black college and university presidents and their role in grooming the next generation of leaders. *Teachers College Record, 116*, 1–34.

For public feedback: A college ratings framework. (2015). https://www.ed.gov/collegeratings.

Freeman, S., Commodore, F., Gasman, M., and Carter, C. (2016). Leaders wanted! The skills expected and needed for a successful 21st century historically Black college and university presidency. *Journal of Black Studies, 47*(6), 570–591.

Freeman, S., and Gasman, M. (2014). The characteristics of historically Black college and university presidents and their role in grooming the next generation of leaders. *Teachers College Record, 116,* 1–34.

Gardner, L. (March 1, 2016). Retired HBCU presidents start search firm for Black-college leaders. *The Chronicle of Higher Education.* https://www.chronicle.com/article/Retired-HBCU-Presidents-Start/235539.

Gasman, M. (2010). *Comprehensive funding approaches for historical Black colleges and Universities.* Philadelphia, PA: University of Pennsylvania, Center of Minority Serving Institutions.

Gasman, M. (September 2, 2016). HBCUs self-imposed leadership struggles. *Inside Higher Ed.* https://www.insidehighered.com/views/2016/09/02/boards-hbcus-should-not-micromanage-their-presidents-essay.

Gasman, M., Lundy-Wagner, V., Ransom, T., and Bowman, N. (2010). Unearthing promise and potential: Our nation's historically Black colleges and universities. *ASHE Higher Education Report, 35*(5), 1–120. San Francisco, CA: Jossey Bass.

Gasman, M., Nguyen, T., Castro Samayoa, A., Commodore, F., and Abiola, U. (2013). *The changing face of historically Black colleges and universities.* Philadelphia, PA: University of Pennsylvania, Center of Minority Serving Institutions.

Harper, S., Patton, L., and Wooden, O. (2009). Access and equity for African American students in higher education: A critical race historical analysis of policy efforts. *The Journal of Higher Education, 80*(4), 389–414.

Hodge-Clark, K., and Daniels, B. (2014). *Top strategic issues facing HBCUs, now and into the future.* A Report by the Association of Governing Boards of Universities and Colleges. https://www.agb.org/sites/default/files/legacy/2014TopStrategicIssuesFacingHBCUs.pdf.

Holmes, S. L. (2004). An overview of African American college presidents: A game of two steps forward, one step backward, and standing still. *Journal of Negro Education, 73*(1), 21–39.

Hefner, D. N. (2014). *Perceptions of transformational and transactional leadership at historically Black colleges and universities.* ProQuest Dissertations & Theses Global (1620540779).

Julius, D. J., Baldridge, J. V., and Pfeffer, J. (1999). A memo from Machiavelli. *Journal of Higher Education, 70*(2), 113–133.

Kimbrough, W. (April 2, 2014). *HBCU presidential crisis: Here's what can be done now.* http://diverseeducation.com/article/62608.

Leadership. (n.d.). https://www.merriam-webster.com/ (accessed April 22, 2017).

LeMelle, T. (2002). The HBCU: Yesterday, today and tomorrow. *Education, 123*(1), 190–197.

Medina, D. A., and Allen, R. (February 27, 2017). What is the future for America's historically Black colleges and universities. *NBC News.* https://www.nbcnews.com/nightly-news/what-future-america-s-historically-black-colleges-universities-n725811.

National Center for Education Statistics. (2016). *Fall enrollment, degrees conferred, and expenditures in degree-granting historically Black colleges and universities,* by institution: *2014, 2015, and 2014–15*. https://nces.ed.gov/programs/digest/d16/tables/dt16_313.10.asp?current=yes.

National Center for Education Statistics. (2017). *Fast facts: Historically Black colleges and universities*. https://nces.ed.gov/fastfacts/display.asp?id=667.

Northouse, P. G. (2013). *Leadership: Theory and practice* (6th ed.). Thousand Oaks, CA: Sage.

Rivard, R. (June 24, 2014). Fighting for survival. *Inside Higher Ed*. https://www.insidehighered.com/news/2014/06/24/public-hbcus-facing-tests-many-fronts-fight-survival.

Schexnider, A. J. (December 20, 2017). Governance and the future of Black colleges. *Inside Higher Ed*. https://www.insidehighered.com/views/2017/12/20/struggling-hbcus-must-consider-new-options-survival-opinion.

Thelin, J. (2004). *A history of American higher education*. Baltimore, MD: Johns Hopkins Press.

Watson, J. E. (July 16, 2017). After four decades on the job, HBCU president has passed the mantle. *Diverse Issues in Higher Education*. http://diverseeducation.com/article/99087.

Williams, M. G. (2016). Increasing philanthropic support through entrepreneurial activities at historically Black colleges and universities. *International Journal of Educational Advancement, 10*(*3*), 216–229.

Willie, C. V., Reddick, R. J., and Brown, R. (2006). *The Black college mystique*. Lanham, MD: Rowman & Littlefield.

*Chapter 4*

# From Conceptualization to Action

## *Academic Program Assessment Opportunities for HBCUs in the Age of Accountability*

### Kimberly Young Walker

## THE NEW AGE OF ACCOUNTABILITY

*Accountability* is one of the new buzz words in higher education. There have been frequent ideological narratives piercing the conversations surrounding higher education such as *performance funding*, *college readiness*, and *student loan debt*. The aforementioned narratives all either lead to—or are an integral part of—the overarching expectation of accountability. It is no longer enough to emphatically state that students on a given campus are learning. There is now an expectation that the "learning" is stated, proven, and measured. Assessment best-practice indicates that true programmatic academic assessment include well-defined student learning outcomes; the collection of data using multiple measures that indicate whether students are achieving that learning outcome; and usage of that data to inform and refine the process. The academic assessment process is considered to be the backbone of *accountability* due to its inherent role in educating students.

Although some scholars go as far as to call accountability conversations a "myth" (Carey, 2007), the recent focus and persistence of this conversation in the academic realm lends credibility to the movement in higher education. It also suggests that calls to action for improving various accountability measures including (a) higher education viability, (b) ensuring quality education, and (c) reducing student debt loads will not cease to happen in the near future (Ciccone, Huber, Hutchings, and Cambridge, 2009; Ewell, 2013; United States Congress Senate Committee on Banking, Housing, and Urban Affairs, 2014). With *accountability* at the forefront of national conversations regarding higher education and the continued development of metrics to measure this accountability, scholars have increasingly turned toward collaboration, meaningful dialogue, and scholarship surrounding the improvement of the student learning aspect, in particular. More specifically, scholars are focusing on the conversations surrounding the inclusion of faculty voices as an integral part of academic assessment processes (Hutchings, 2010).

## ACCOUNTABILITY AND THE HBCU

The focus on *accountability* and academic assessment can be perceived as more acute on historically Black college and university (HBCU) campuses. With more than 20 percent of African Americans who receive degrees being educated at HBCUs (Thurgood Marshall College Fund, n.d.) it is fair to say that their academic assessment processes are important for the overall success of African American college graduates. Additionally, HBCUs have received the reputation (whether fair or not) of providing educational rigor that are less than those of their predominantly White institutions (PWI) counterparts. One way to provide evidence to the contrary would be to prove the rigor of the curriculum and educational experiences through appropriate best-practice academic assessment.

Another avenue to be explored is the continual concern and peril of HBCUs in relation to accrediting bodies. An effective systematic assessment process is essential to the successful accreditation efforts of HBCUs. Administrators on campus assert that the accreditation process is important, however, they may fail to understand the extent to which this process involves multiple individuals and countless hours invested. In addition, concepts that were previously only associated with institution level academic assessment are now being considered in the *Performance Funding* conversations of governing bodies (Jones, 2014). If these assertions are to be viewed through broad lenses it reveals that the importance of academic assessment is understood in relation to successful accreditation (Beld, 2013), however, the process of a systematic ongoing effort (continuous improvement) may be lost in translation. This means that academic assessment—whether related to accreditation or not—cannot be an episodic venture that is instituted prior to an impending accreditation visit but a continual process that is used to improve the learning that is taking place on a campus rather than a rushed effort to fulfill externally imposed requirements.

Moreover, the notion that *culture matters* leads to a unique issue for HBCUs. It is quite possible that academic assessment best-practice transcends the type of institution; however, the research literature that focuses on assessment in HBCUs is slim. This means that institutions will be forced to create their own processes with little in the way of literature as a guiding post. This could, potentially, be great news. The idea that HBCUs can create their own way in academic assessment planning without attempting to mimic the previously asserted notions of PWIs could be the openness necessary to usher in culturally competent assessment that is not forced to fit into previously established notions of acceptability. This is especially important when HBCU faculty express concerns with having the appropriate amount of time to conduct academic assessments of substance (Jones, 2010). An opportunity to reinvent the academic assessment processes as we know it may be exactly what HBCUs need to elevate their current assessment processes to a level that completely negates previously conceived notions about rigor and shifts accreditation visits from frantic to welcomed due to existing systematic assessments already in place.

## ACADEMIC PROGRAM ASSESSMENT INTEGRATION

Academic program assessment is normally perceived as a bureaucratic exercise by faculty members who are expected to step in and create academic assessment processes that appropriately incorporate assessment best-practice, often, with little or no training. There are a number of recommendations regarding how to appropriately and effectively orient faculty to academic assessment planning (Palomba and Banta, 1999), however, it is up to institutional leadership to encourage and insist that these recommendations are heeded and implemented. In the absence of that focus and support lies an opportunity for collaboration and a different type of leadership that extends beyond positional power.

The National Institute for Learning Outcomes Assessment (NILOA) recently published a document that explicitly outlines the importance of academic assessment (Higher Education Quality, 2016). The third point states, "Collaborate with the relevant stakeholders, beginning with the faculty." Although this is a relatively new perspective of assessment in higher education, it is becoming more common in the literature as many universities attempt to integrate accountability expectations in alignment with their institutional missions while ensuring that faculty perspectives are central to the conversation (Association of American Colleges and Universities, 2008). Moreover, when faculty have an audible and welcomed voice in the academic assessment process the overt hostility that is noted between faculty and assessment staff is significantly reduced (Ciccone, Huber, Hutchings, and Cambridge, 2009).

## ADMINISTRATIVE ACCOUNTABILITY

This new move toward accountability has placed college administrators (presidents, provosts, and deans) on notice. They now have a distinct role to play in academics beyond leading the institution from broader perspectives of lobbying, fundraising, collaborating, or researching. Individuals formerly believed to be "figureheads" of a university or college are now expected to be able to confidently speak to the learning that is taking place within their colleges and universities. They must account for this learning via reports that are due to state and federal stakeholders in addition to their routine regional accreditation review. Although the campus leadership may not aggregate the data, author the reports, or fact-check the information, there is an expectation that they be aware and responsive to the educational needs of their students and react in timely and responsible ways.

At this juncture, the call to leadership is one *from* assessment scholars and staff *to* administrative positional leadership for the necessary inclusion of faculty perspectives when developing the academic assessment planning processes that will undoubtedly influence the accountability conversations. Positional leadership is different from leadership built on trust and value (Northouse, 2010). Additionally, positional leadership is widely considered to be the lowest form of leadership (Maxwell, 2011), therefore, assessment experts have taken it upon themselves to model the necessary leadership that will appropriately include faculty voices in hopes that the success of these endeavors will eventually elicit the buy-in from those with positional power. The idea is to be prepared and aware as the accountability conversation evolve to inevitably include academic assessment planning which will include the measurement of student learning outcomes by default and to prompt a response from leadership prior to a crisis arising at the institution.

## FROM CONCEPTUALIZATION TO ACTION

As assessment becomes an integral part of higher education and moves to the forefront of accountability conversations, it is imperative that the academic assessment process reflects the values of the not only the institution, but the individual schools and colleges as well (Middaugh, 2010). One way to ensure the institutional academic assessment process has buy-in from faculty stakeholders is by incorporating their opinions, being receptive to suggestions, and valuing content knowledge as an essential aspect of institutional academic assessment (Palomba and Banta, 1999). There are firsthand accounts of the positive outcomes of incorporating faculty voices in academic assessment planning that lead to positive attention from administrative figures.

While an assessment professional staff member at a southern research university I was able to overcome the perceived adversarial relationship between faculty and institutional assessment staff. In an effort to create a more effective and collaborative process, the institution's official office for academic assessment had created an assessment plan feedback review process that entailed ongoing one-on-one sessions with various faculty members in order to review academic assessment plans that were submitted annually to the office for review (see figure 4.1).

The one-on-one feedback sessions generally required ten to twelve weeks to complete per college. During these meetings the faculty liaison and assessment professional would share information regarding their respective areas of expertise. Faculty were able to give feedback regarding whether assignments were appropriate given the course and learning outcomes. And more often than not, the individual was a familiar colleague to the broader college faculty, thus, becoming a trusted intermediary. Moreover, the faculty member acted as a liaison to departmental faculty who had direct contact with the data and students. This helped ensure that data was not only timely, but also accurate. The assessment professional was able to provide feedback on assessment best-practice as it related to providing appropriate data and usage of data; ensuring that learning outcomes met a basic standard; including appropriate curriculum information; defining acceptable measures and criteria; and confirming that the data was being shared with the appropriate individuals on a regular basis.

Through this exploration I found that a faculty member was integral in providing academic assessment planning that was appropriate for each school or college. This process was a collaborative effort that positively impacted students and programs (figure 4.2). Working with faculty who were content knowledge experts revealed areas of improvement within academic program assessment on that campus including how the office could include more

Figure 4.1   Annual Academic Assessment Review Process.

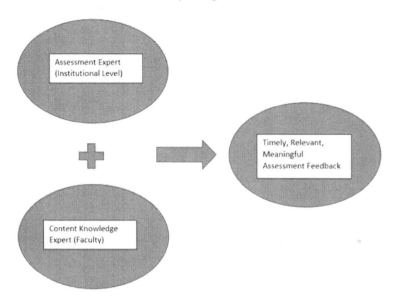

**Figure 4.2    Ideally, assessment staff and content knowledge experts can combine specific areas of expertise in order to properly vet learning outcomes, measures, and ensure appropriate utilization of results.**

faculty voices, what types of assessment cycles are helpful to programs and colleges, and what types of assessment professional development is most needed (Maki, 2010). Additionally, faculty liaisons developed working relationships with other faculty across campus.

When the faculty liaisons were contacted regarding the implementation of academic program assessment collaboration, the faculty explained that the interactions were meaningful, targeted, and easily understood without need for subjective interpretation (see figure 4.2). Having direct feedback reduced time spent on interpreting rubrics and comments. Some content knowledge experts worked tirelessly for weeks with faculty members to retrieve data and appropriate academic assessment plans in order to encourage timely updates. The aforementioned collaboration created an advocate for academic assessment who then was able to share and expound upon those experiences with college deans and assistant deans. The assessment office on the campus utilized that faculty member's positive experience to encourage other faculty members to take advantage of opportunities to learn about assessment and implement these ideas in their colleges.

Additionally, having a faculty member who appreciated the assessment staff's work gave the office not only credibility among other faculty, but it also encouraged faculty to work with the office going forward to implement more appropriate academic assessment activities within their schools and colleges. By the end of this process, four additional faculty members from different colleges were willing to be trained on the assessment best-practice methods used in order to create academic assessment planning strategies within their own colleges. They were prepared to implement their own process for their college using the aforementioned experience as a guiding post.

When faced with continuing issues of compliance, the assessment office decided to pursue an integrative approach that began with faculty stakeholders because they realized the concerns began and ended with the faculty members who were an essential part of the academic assessment process at every phase—and they absolutely needed to be a vocal stakeholder in the step of this process that happens at the institutional level. In truth, the overarching success of this "grass roots" process was unexpected, but welcomed. These efforts were "grass roots" in that it started with assessment staff and not the administrative leadership. Ideally, this process would have started with administrative leaders realizing that the age of accountability in higher education had arrived and began to disseminate support of academic assessment efforts. Since the effort started at lower levels within the institution, it necessitated a collaborative approach that considered the buy-in and consideration of all interested (and uninterested) parties.

When training other faculty members on assessment best-practice, the assessment of academic learning becomes a formidable partnership of individuals who are most well positioned to have positive impacts. Faculty have direct contact with the students and can, therefore, make timely adjustments to their assessment processes. Additionally, faculty have in-depth understandings of particular content areas. Assessment staff understand how best to track student learning outcomes and "close the loop." This combination of faculty's content expertise and assessment expertise built upon trust and inclusion has succeeded in making the first step of creating a culture of faculty lead academic assessment planning.

There are several aspects of this process that needs to be considered by institutions that seek to seamlessly integrate university level academic assessment into existing educational processes in a meaningful and useful way. The first is to examine the existing academic assessment structure. Due to academic assessment planning falling into a pattern of bureaucratic exercise, the assessment process can be an addendum to existing educational processes (see figure 4.3) instead of being appropriately integrated (see figure 4.4).

The endeavor of incorporating faculty voices in academic assessment plans as liaisons and leaders is one that will require resources and time in the form of (a) dedicated and interested faculty liaisons, (b) collaborative relationship

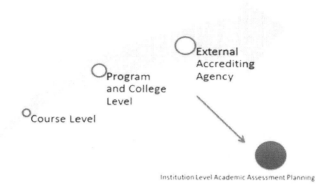

Institution Level Academic Assessment Planning

**Figure 4.3  The Existing Structure of Institution Level Academic Assessment Planning Has Created a Process by Which Assessment Planning Becomes an Aside, or Bureaucratic Exercise, Rather Than a Properly Integrated Aspect of Existing Educational Processes within a College.**

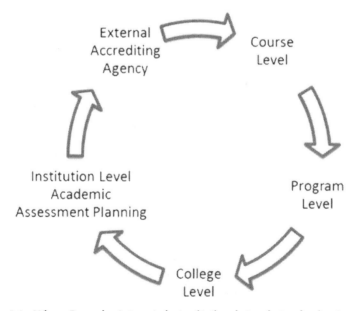

**Figure 4.4  When Properly Integrated, Institutional Level Academic Assessment Planning Can Flow Seamlessly through the Existing Educational Processes.**

between assessment staff and faculty built on trust and understanding so that faculty can be trained on assessment best-practice, and (c), most importantly, positional leaders providing institutional buy-in and support. Tailoring each and every assessment process based on the academic unit is time consuming at best and a strain on resources at worst. These tasks are daunting but necessary. There has to be tangible effort on the part of assessment staff to foster meaningful relationships with faculty campus partners who are intimately involved with their department's assessment processes. David Grossman (2011) states it very plainly when discussing what it means to be an assessment professional in a relationship with a faculty member. Grossman describes a "relationship" called "symbiosis," meaning, our academic assessment processes need to be beneficial for everyone involved. Although faculty and assessment staff are "two different species" who have two very different goals in mind, it would be beneficial to both if there is some intentionality behind the assessment processes that are currently implemented in higher education.

This process was not easy, quick, nor painless because it was a paradigm shift for assessment on this campus. There are those who have no desire to improve the departmental assessment process because it is an addendum to the work that they are already required to do as a faculty member. It is not an essential part of their duties, they do not want it to be and, therefore, it will never be. However, assessment staff, faculty liaisons, and ultimately administrators still have to work with those individuals in an attempt to improve upon what already exists. One way to work with faculty is to convince them of the importance of what they are doing in regard to the university as a whole including university accreditation.

The aforementioned process is a firsthand account of the potential for meaningful academic assessment planning at the institutional level. However, this process has the capacity to change the culture of an institution if the institutional leadership decides that the *accountability* culture being realized across the United States is deserving of attention. Arguably, the number one mission of any postsecondary institution should include the learning of its students at the core. If that is the case, it is only a matter of time before this "grass roots" effort of assessment staff and a few dedicated faculty become the center of *accountability* conversations at institutions across the nations.

It can be helpful for those who are in direct contact with the day-to-day operations to have a facilitating conversation to enable the process to begin. While adjusting the academic program assessment at the aforementioned institution I began to outline the process as I went through to help frame the experience. See figure 4.5 for the scaffolding exercise that will help assessment staff at institutions appropriately incorporate faculty perspectives through conceptualization of current and ideal practices (see figures 4.6, 4.7, and 4.8)

**Pre-Plan Part A:**

What is the first word or phrase that comes to your mind when you think about faculty involvement with institutional academic program assessment? Why was ____ your first thought? In what ways has your campus climate impacted your answer?

**Pre-Plan Part B:**

What opportunities exist on your campus to get faculty voices involved in the assessment process? (Examples include HR sponsored workshops, faculty development centers, faculty meetings as a guest speaker, etc.)

**Figure 4.5 The initial conceptualization of assessment processes should be an analysis of the current process.**

**Plan of Action**

Title:

**Part One-A:**

**Identify the following:**

Stakeholders:

Allies (who may be willing to assist in the transition):

Holdouts (who will resist the transition):

**Part One-B:**

Using illustrations, demonstrate your current academic assessment process then illustrate how you envision the academic assessment processes functioning with faculty input.

Current Process

Faculty Inclusive Process

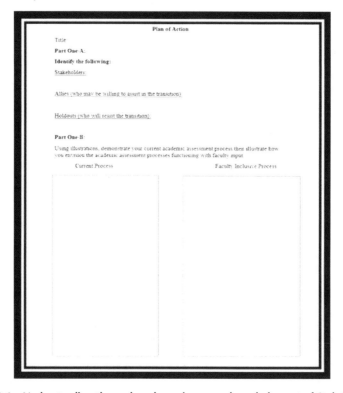

**Figure 4.6 Understanding the end goal requires an acknowledgment of Stakeholders, Allies, Holdouts, and the ultimate desires of the institution.**

**Figure 4.7  Acknowledgement of academic differences across colleges in the initial analysis can save time at the end of the process.** By doing so, the process is inclusive in its inception and can create buy-in.

**Figure 4.8  The ultimate plan of action can be adjusted throughout the process to account for unexpected occurences.**

# BIBLIOGRAPHY

Association of American Colleges and Universities (AAC&U). (2008). *Our students' best work: A framework for accountability worthy of our mission* (2nd ed.). Washington, DC: Author.

Beld, J. M. (2013). *Advancing excellence, enhancing equity: Making the case for assessment at Minority-Serving Institutions.* A report published by the Southern Education Foundation, Atlanta, GA.

Carey, K. (September/October 2007). Truth without action: The myth of higher-education accountability. *Change, 39*(5), 24–29.

Ciccone, A., Huber, M. T., Hutchings, P., and Cambridge, B. (2009). Exploring impact: A survey of participants in the CASTL institutional leadership and affiliates program. Unpublished paper, The Carnegie Foundation for the Advancement of Teaching, Stanford, CA.

Grossman, D. (2011). The relationship of the researcher with faculty in assessing student learning. Unpublished Paper, Academic Senate for California Community Colleges. Retrieved from: http://www.asccc.org/content/relationship-researcher-faculty-assessing-student-learning.

Hutchings, P. (April 2010). Opening doors to faculty involvement in assessment. (Occasional Paper No. 4). Urbana, IL: University of Illinois and Indiana University, National Institute for Learning Outcomes Assessment.

Jones, T. (2014). *Performance funding at MSIs: Considerations and possible measures for public minority-serving institutions.* A report published by the Southern Education, Foundation, Atlanta, GA.

Jones, W. (2010). General education assessment at private historically Black colleges a universities: An exploratory study. *The Journal of General Education, 59*(1), 1–16.

Maki, P. (2010). *Assessing for learning.* Sterling, VA: Stylus Publishing, LLC.

Maxwell, J. C. (2011). *The 5 levels of leadership.* New York: Center Street.

Middaugh, M. (2010). *Planning and assessment in higher education: Demonstrating institutional effectiveness.* San Francisco, CA: Jossey Bass.

National Institute for Learning Outcomes Assessment (NILOA). (May 2016). *Higher education quality: Why documenting learning matters, A policy statement from the national institute for learning outcomes assessment.* Urbana, IL: University of Illinois and Indiana University, Author.

Northouse, P. (2010). *Leadership: Theory and practice.* Thousand Oaks, CA: Sage Publication.

Palomba, C., and Banta, T. (1999). *Assessment essentials: Planning, implementing, and improving assessment in higher education.* San Francisco, CA: Jossey Bass.

Thurgood Marshall College Fund. (n.d.). *About us.* https://tmcf.org/about-us/our-schools/hbcus.

United States Congress Senate Committee on Banking, Housing, and Urban Affairs. (2014). *Financial products for students: Issues and challenges: Hearing before the committee on banking, housing, and urban affairs, United States senate, one hundred thirteenth congress, second session, on examining issues related to financial institutions and postsecondary education, including private student loans, student loan servicing, student loan debt collection, and refund balance cards.* Washington, DC: US Government Publishing Office.

*Chapter 5*

# Public Relations with Purpose

## *Opportunities for HBCU Leaders to Control the Narrative*

### Maquisha Mullins

The value of the education historically Black colleges or universities (HBCUs) provide is commonly questioned. Are the longstanding HBCUs still relevant? Are these institutions able to provide the diversity African American students require for success? Will graduates have the skills to be competent professionals? These are a few of the questions that are openly debated in American culture permeating messaging that is issued through entertainment media, journalistic outlets, ranking organizations, and directly from HBCUs. Examination is warranted in establishing if current messaging is following the historically negative narrative regarding HBCUs. It is possible current messages dominating mainstream discourse are using a more balanced sample of HBCUs, drawing from those that are highly acclaimed and those that may receive less notoriety.

## FOUNDATION OF THE HBCU NARRATIVE

According to the traditionally Black institutions of higher education report published in 1982 by the National Center for Education Statistics, "TBIs had a great impact on the progress made by Blacks to improve their status in the United States." The list of 105 TBIs were defined as those established prior to 1954, the year of the Brown vs. Board of education decision, which legally mandated the desegregation of public education. These institutions were credited in the report for training the majority of Black doctors, lawyers, dentists, and teachers in the United States (Hill, 1982).

The first public university in the United States, the University of North Carolina at Chapel Hill officially opened its doors on January 15, 1795 (Carolina Story: Virtual Museum of University History, 2004). The first student of the university Hinton James arrived on February 12, when Blacks were not allowed to attend. As time went on UNC resisted the attempts of African American students to attend the school until a federal court ruling in 1951 ordered the UNC to admit African American students to its graduate programs at the law and medical schools. A separate court order in 1955 forced the university to begin admitting African American undergraduate students. This example highlights that the establishment of public higher education institutions in America was never intended to serve Blacks and Whites jointly (Carolina Story: Virtual Museum of University History, 2004).

The exclusion of Blacks from higher education required separate institutions to be established. The inception of the first HBCU placed it in an environment that was hostile to the advancement of African Americans. Predating the Civil War, Lincoln University was established in Pennsylvania in 1854 by members of the Presbyterian Church. The Civil War highlighted the great divide in America with regard to slavery as the top economic and moral issue of the period. During this time Blacks were legally, as well as by social constraints, forbidden from learning or being taught to read or write. However, post–Civil War America allowed many different private groups the opportunity to begin to invest in African American education. Much of the effort came from the Black community itself, churches in the Northern states, freedmen's societies, and philanthropists. During reconstruction in America, there was also the creation of state-funded public education for Blacks and Whites in the form of primary and secondary schools. These lower-level institutions were needed because the majority of African Americans during that period did not receive much formal education. Some schools later expanded their offerings to include college-level curricula (Hill, 1982).

Current criticism of the role and contributions of HBCUs dishonors the historical context that mandated the birth of these institutions. Under external pressure, many, not all, leaders of HBCUs miss opportunities to tell the story of their institution a priority, by failing to weave it into the organizational culture. A review of institutional websites reveals few vice president level positions designated for communications professionals. Placement of public relations practitioners in the leadership team of the university keeps a spotlight on maintaining the critical relationships of the institution and carefully crafted messaging.

Many news stories about majority Black colleges highlight the downfalls, failings, and missteps by administrators (Riley, 2010) (see figure 5.1). Public relations practitioners should be empowered to reframe the conversation, expressing HBCU's ability to innovate and augment offerings as their students' needs for a higher level of challenge increased. It might be added to the conversation that HBCUs are only 4 percent (figure 5.2) of all colleges in

**Typical University Administrative Organization**

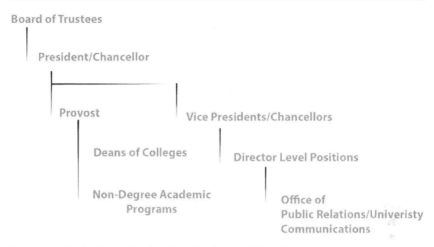

Figure 5.1   Typical organization of university administration.

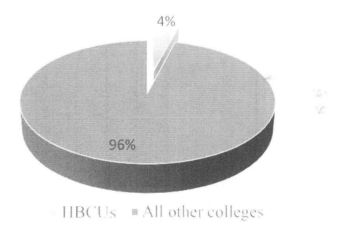

Figure 5.2   The percentage of US colleges that are HBCUs.

the United States, but enroll 10 percent of African American college students, confer 21 percent of bachelor's degrees and 24 percent of science, technology, engineering, and math (STEM) degrees, and out of all colleges and universities across the United States consistently produce 24 percent of African American graduate professionals (United Negro College Fund, 2017). The current statistics about these accomplishments should be used broadly by HBCUs to dispel misperceptions [McCee, 2008]).

## Media Usage of HBCUs

The conduction of an initial database search of a newswire, Global News-stream using keyword *historically Black colleges and universities* yielded 440 headlines of news items related to HBCUs from January 1, 2018, to March 8, 2018. The items include features, opinion editorials, events, and news columns. The articles were divided into two categories of positive or negative headlines. Headlines that mentioned school closings, financial woes, or criminal acts that occur on campus are categorized as negative. A headline receiving a positive designation includes subject matter that is somewhat benign with regard to the reputation of the institution, or HBCUs as a whole: student achievements, faculty achievements, athletics, special events, and so on. Within the total number of search results, it was determined that 220 were directly related to HBCUs. From the 220 HBCU headlines, only 9 were categorized as overtly negative (i.e., failing institutions). In the 211 positive headlines, there were 105 items that were attributed to an HBCU or an organization officially representing HBCUs, such as the UNCF (figure 5.2).

More HBCU public relations (PR) offices could benefit from the opportunities newswires provide, releasing information to a newswire for a major story that could be of interests to news outlets all over the world. Everyday news outlets are seeking information on a variety of topics that millions of people will read in newspapers, hear on the radio, read online, and watch on television news. Researchers have approximated that 40 percent to 70 percent of the news covered is the result of PR efforts (Lattimore, Baskin, Heiman, and Toth, 2012). Subscribers to wire services are an audience the average HBCU would not have direct access to, but is looking for expert input. Communications professionals at HBCUs will be well served by taking the time to compile a database of the key individuals within their university that are readily available to share their subject matter expertise. Remaining abreast of the latest patents, awards and cutting-edge research produced by members of their university community will bolster the work of building the university's reputation. To accomplish this, practitioners will invest in educating the faculty, staff and students, about how they may contribute to the PR efforts of the university when a journalist requests an interview, insight, or information. Monitoring journalists' requests may be accomplished through the use of services such as ProfNet (an affiliate of PRNewsWire) for high profile events, or announcements (Lattimore et al., 2012). There is an expense related to using each of these services, so it is important that PR offices establish the appropriate infrastructure prior to subscribing to the service so the maximum benefit may be received.

Though there are many great services and technological shortcuts available to PR professionals, there is no replacement for traditional media relations, establishing professional relationships with key media figures. A quality relationship with the media means providing newsworthy information with varying levels of interest, local, national and international, while furthering the agenda of the institution. A PR person may influence the pleasant tone of a story by being pleasant and helpful to writers (Wilcox, Cameron, Ault, and Agee, 2003).

Keeping the progress and accomplishments of HBCUs at the forefront of higher education is a formidable task for PR professionals. The use of controlled media, or media formats without third-party gatekeepers, is paramount to advance the institution's message, and gain control of their narrative. A newsletter, website, or blog are customizable and information may be updated as frequently as the public it is created to reach demands—customizing it with the types of information desired.

A study of HBCUs' internet presence assessed the homepages of institutions' websites based on factors such as prestige, student information, athletics, faculty, alumni, institutional news, branding, and fundraising. Brunner and Broyer (2008) found that of the 96 institutions with websites, 19.5 percent highlighted information about rankings issued by either *US News & World Report*, Tom Joyner, or *Princeton Review*. Nearly 20 percent of websites showcased news of public relations items about current students. Only 12.5 percent of sites featured information about their athletic programs. Faculty accomplishments were represented on 10.4 percent of sites and only 4.2 percent offered information about alumni accomplishments. There were links to giving opportunities on 20.8 percent of sites. A more encouraging finding was that 51 percent of the websites offered news, or public relations items. Unfortunately, much of what was shared at the time of study proved to be old stories; 18.8 percent had stories that were 1 to 3 months old, stories that were 4 to 6 months old were found on 4.2 percent of sites and 2.1 percent of websites presented stories 10 or more months old (Brunner and Boyer, 2008).

Opening the lines of communication with the news media is important for the augmentation of PR efforts at HBCUs. A review of what is considered the ten highest ranked and the ten lowest ranked, as defined by *US News & World Report* (2018), HBCUs' websites, one may infer that interaction with the press is a low priority. Only 20 percent of the websites reviewed have links for the media on the homepage. There is a difference when one compares the two categories of colleges, 40 percent of the high-ranking institutions compared with 0 percent of low ranking, or unranked colleges, have dedicated an area of the website for a pressroom. Having a pressroom on the website is a simple means of providing the media with access to university experts and the opportunity to request institutional information.

An institution-controlled website presents the perfect opportunity for an HBCU to present strong positive images that showcase the brand for its primary publics. It is unfortunate that only 11.5 percent of the universities capitalized on the opportunity presented when a visitor's initial interaction with a website homepage to brand itself. The descriptions used were leader (3.1 percent), progressive (2.1 percent), and student centered (6.3 percent). Descriptive terms such as these are able to connect with the virtual visitors and encourage them to go deeper into the sites (Brunner and Broyer, 2008). In the twenty-first century, an online presence can be uniquely crafted to provide information to perspective and current students, alumni, connect with donors, and engage media outlets. Each of these groups requires unique public relations efforts to develop and retain their interests in, and positive attitudes about, the university.

## Connecting to Current Students and Alumni

It is noted that the majority of attendees of HBCUs enjoy their undergraduate experiences and sing the praises of their institutions (McCee, 2008; Petrie, 2007). This devotion seems to persist in a media environment that may be considered hostile to HBCUs questioning whether the colleges are useful in the present educational environment where African Americans can attend predominately White institutions, (PWIs), if they so choose (Riley, 2010). So what messages are HBCUs delivering to students to reassure them that they made the right choice and what is unique about the collegiate experience on the HBCU campus?

HBCU attendees select their school as a result of legacy, and often because of a connection to the original reason it was established, to educate and provide opportunities to elevate African Americans and their families from the extreme poverty the enslavement of Africans created. Students are still able to relate to the ideal of education as a method to move ahead in life and secure, or solidify, a place in the middle class of America (Hill, 1982). Though the campuses are steeped in historic movements, the social aspects of the college experience are not lost on students. The opportunity to join one of the African American fraternities or sororities, the homecoming celebrations, and halftime shows ostentatiously provided by the marching band is appealing to many, but is it enough for students (Petrie, 2007)?

On higher education campuses, students may express frustration with their treatment as students or policies while demanding that administrators value their voices. Often this discontent will not outweigh the positive emotions connected with the individual college experience; friendships forged, spring break trips, and game time chants. There is something exceptional occurring on HBCU campuses. In a 2011 study, students clearly express the sense of cultural empowerment that their HBCU provides, insulating them from racial biases in daily classroom interactions. Guiding students' choices is the sense of family and belonging they receive that is unique to the HBCU campus experience for African Americans. On an HBCU campus, Black students rarely wonder if the institution is a place for them because the institution was established to provide academic opportunity and emotional support for African Americans. The sentiments student participants in the study convey echo across the over one hundred HBCU campuses. PR offices must highlight these attributes to attract new students and reinforce the positive attitudes toward the institution of current students and remind alumni of their fondness for their alma mater (Awokoya and Mann, 2011).

The African American alumni of HBCUs report feeling that their alma mater prepared them well for life after college at 55 percent, compared to 29 percent of their non-HBCU graduate counterparts. HBCU graduates report being engaged at work at a rate of 39 percent compared to 33 percent of non-HBCU attendees. In the Gallup-USA Funds Minority College Graduates Report graduates of HBCUs state having at least one professor that made them excited to learn, cared about them as people and having a mentor who encouraged them to pursue their goals (Gallup, 2015). A plausible transition from this positive sentiment is to empower alumni as natural extensions of a university's PR office in fundraising, advocacy efforts by writing opinion editorials in newspapers, or blog entries for institutional websites.

## Focused Fundraising Efforts

Fundraising is a critical aspect of public relations that institutions cannot afford to neglect. Before many private HBCUs were able to receive federal funds of any type (student loans, grants, etc.), there was a reliance on private donors from African American churches, the founding organization, philanthropists, and the attendees'—largely hailing from middle-class families—ability to pay fees out of pocket (Hill, 1982). The initial scholarly interpretation of the philanthropy of wealthy industrialists post-Civil War was that it was all altruist generosity. There were also scholars that presented the view of philanthropists, many wealthy industrialists, as being self-serving and attempting to retain control of the southern labor force (Gasman and Drezner, 2009). Few empirical studies have been conducted including HBCUs, and even fewer focusing on fundraising by HBCUs. With an eye on sustainability, PR professionals have to take great care in connecting with existing and possible donors. The creation of advancement, or development, offices shows universities recognize the importance of managing the relationships with donors (Tindall, 2007).

There are four primary models applied by PR professionals in managing relationships, established by the research team Grunig, Grunig, and Hunt. The models are press agentry/publicity, public information, two-way asymmetrical, and two-way symmetrical (Lattimore et al., 2012). In the fulfillment of the fundraising function of most charitable organizations, the press agentry model is frequently employed. The use of publicity as the primary approach to fundraising means an organization is simply announcing its cause and soliciting financial contributions. A more sophisticated approach is the two-symmetrical model where donors are not only solicited for their financial contributions, but also there is more interaction and dialogue that may draw the donor into active participation (i.e., planning events, chairing committees) on behalf of the organization. However, the latter requires a larger number of staff members, stretching departmental budgets, which increases fiscal demands on the HBCU (Gasman and Drezner, 2010; Tindall, 2007).

In terms of the HBCUs in Tindall's study (2007), it unearthed factors that were strongly associated with the type of fundraising model that is used at an HBCU. A key factor identified by the study is the educational level of the practitioners. The greater the educational level of a practitioner the less likely the practitioner is to practice press agentry as a fundraising model, instead using alternative techniques. The researcher found that a practitioner's age is also related to the practice of two-way symmetrical models in fundraising, showing younger practitioners choosing to implement this approach in conjunction with the one-way publicity approach heavily relied upon by older practitioners.

Researchers in a 2010 article "Fundraising for Black Colleges During the 1960s and 1970s: The Case of Hampton Institute" explore the story of Hampton University's fundraising trials and triumphs (Gasman and Drezner, 2009). In 1968, the then Hampton Institute boldly decided to separate from the United Negro College Fund, a fundraising organization dedicated to the support of private HBCUs. This pivotal decision came some years after the 1954 Brown vs. Board of education decision and Hampton was actively asserting its relevancy to funders though Blacks were able to integrate PWIs. Upon parting ways with the UNCF, Hampton enlisted the professional guidance of another proven fundraiser for HBCUs, the Oram Group, which is credited with a level of success only second to the UNCF.

Once hired, the Oram Group performed an assessment, made several predictions and suggestions to the university: to increase the contribution burden of the board of trustees to 20 percent from less than 1 percent; modify the board structure to include individuals that network with people and organizations of means; institute a campaign using a solicitation letter and brochure with a cohesive message of uplifting students; shift annual fundraising goals anticipating 55 percent in the form of individual gifts and 45 percent from foundations and corporations; and lastly, invest in the fundraising personnel and infrastructure of the university to continue procuring alumni donations.

Unlike some of its peers, all of the advice Hampton received it followed and vigilantly executed.

Initially, all of Hampton's fundraising goals were not met, but fifty years later, it possesses an over $279 million endowment. Hampton took control of its financial future by developing intentional messaging around its historical and current contributions to society, to Blacks, and unapologetically garnering financial support from alumni, faculty, staff, and friends of the institution. One may ascertain that much of Hampton's success lies in its discipline and commitment to targeted public relations efforts, as well as in its willingness to invest in the infrastructure that makes it all possible (Gasman and Drezner, 2009).

Small office sizes and lower budgets may not be the only reasons that HBCUs opt for the use of a publicity model for fundraising efforts; it may also be a way of guarding their image. One-way messaging disallows input or influence from the public in which you are communicating. Using this model, an HBCU is able to block heavy criticism from outside entities and display the many positives of its institution. This permits media focus to be placed on new initiatives, or thriving academic programs. While there are a relatively small number of studies on fundraising at HBCUs, this research is ambiguous as to whether HBCUs are intentionally engaging in one-way PR methodologies designed to retain control, or are defaulting to traditional approaches due to limited resources (Tindall, 2007). The accomplishments of Hampton University display how the shifts in funding and the political climate require development efforts to evolve overtime to meet the fiscal demands of an institution (Gasman and Drezner, 2009).

## The Influence of Entertainment Media Imagery

Though largely unencumbered by HBCUs, the representation of university life through entertainment media imagery had an undeniable influence on the perception and renewed interest in attending an all-Black college. *The Cosby Show* which was on air from 1984 to 1992 introduced the fictitious Hillman College to audiences and promoted the virtues of the HBCU through Cliff and Claire Huxtable's joyous recollections of their college days, reconnecting with college classmates and eventually with the spin off *A Different World* (Mcclure, 2011). *A Different World* then carried the mantle of promoting the benefits of attending an HBCU by displaying students of varying socioeconomic levels, high achievers, STEM students, social activists, social networking and intergenerational relationships all on a campus that was grounded in Black consciousness and self-awareness (Luckie, 2015; Mcclure, 2011). During the period, the show was captivating young audiences. There was also Spike Lee's depiction of a Black college experience in the 1988 film *School*

*Daze*. The film was called honest and revealing by respected film critic Roger Ebert for its exploration of activism, classism, and colorism on majority Black campuses (Ebert, 1988).

The preceding examples are not cited to suggest that pop culture should attempt to duplicate these successful and historic media moments. However, it requires a pensive review of what was accomplished through the positive portrayals of student achievement and life on the campus of HBCU. While airing these sitcoms and film were watched by millions of viewers (*The Cosby Show* averaged a weekly audience of 13 million). The ability to harness the power of mass media for the collective good of Black colleges deserves empirical investigation. It has been established that from 1984 to 1993 college enrollment in the United States increased by 16.8 percent, while HBCU enrollment increased by 24.3 percent, equaling about a 44.5 percent better increase than higher education overall. By 2004, just over a decade after the conclusion of the shows and fifteen years post Spike Lee's film, college and university attendance in America grew by 20.7 percent while HBCUs grew by 9.2 percent, approximately 55.5 percent less growth than experienced by US higher education. The enrollment statistics coupled with the timeline shows an association of positive media messaging with higher levels of enrollment in HBCUs (Luckie, 2015; Mcclure, 2011).

Since the 1980s and 1990s cannot be relived, many have written and pondered the question, "Is there a way to use present day mass media to reignite the passion for Black colleges that had been rekindled during the 1980s and 1990s?" Perhaps a modern collegiate experience portrayal via a YouTube channel or utilizing live streaming on Facebook could be employed. Harnessing the contemporary version of television programming, fictitious or not, to capture the spirit of campus life for college-bound youth could be a powerful tool for HBCUs. Millennials are now connecting with *A Different World*, reviving its popularity, purchasing show memorabilia, accessing it through Amazon's streaming service and previously through Netflix. The future will reveal if viewership of the show in a new era yields similar results for HBCUs (Luckie, 2015).

## PRessing the Institution Forward

Ultimately, if all remaining HBCUs are to survive another century and continue to produce graduates that make integral contributions to society, each must invest in the communications aspect of the college. The public relations professionals have an obligation to continue telling and retelling the stories of the great accomplishments that are rooted in their institutions. Effective PR in higher education means prioritizing media relations, community relations, student/alumni relations, and fundraising efforts. Institutions with small staff will have special attention given to where the maximum return on investment may be received. Gaining third-party endorsements are key to successful public relations plans.

The following are recommendations that may be adapted by HBCUs of varying sizes and operating budgets to improve PR efforts.

1. *PR on the leadership team.* PR practitioners at HBCUs must be recognized as critical decision makers and integral parts of university leadership teams. Wherever the communications function is housed within the institution, it has the significant task of managing the image and public regard for the college (Figure 5.3).
2. *Assess the ROI of campaigns* and designate staff members to evaluate and manage the data.
3. *Provide all university community members with consistent information* about the accomplishments of faculty, staff, current students, and graduates. This will reinforce their positive attitudes about *their* university.
4. *Maintain open dialogue with students* utilizing town halls, focus groups, or surveys that permit the ideas and suggestions to be woven into the culture of the university. Transparency in the reporting of data and its application are important.
5. *Study the best practices of and receive counsel from PR professionals at institutions that excel* in areas of PR that your institution is focusing on improving (i.e., Hampton University's and Spelman College's approaches to fundraising).
6. *Engage the community surrounding the institution.* Whether it is in the form of service learning projects or faculty lectures, performing arts events or other activities that engage the surrounding community spur news coverage and public interest.

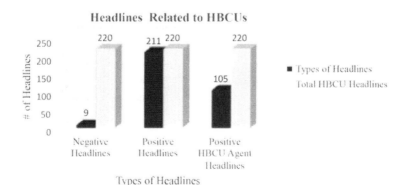

**Figure 5.3   Headlines in early 2018 reflect positive and negative stories on HBCUs.**

7. *Create an online pressroom.* HBCUs should make important newsworthy information available to journalists. If a media link is present on the homepage of the website information and interview requests will be easy to submit. A news release archive and PR office contact information will be readily accessible.

The conversation about maintaining control of the narrative does not mean that only the good things about HBCUs are permitted in the discussion or covered by the media. The role of the media in society is to provide factual information so that there is transparency, but it seems that more negative information about HBCUs reaches national media outlets while positive news remains local. Black colleges should be in continual pursuit of excellence in higher education. Where there is true excellence there also exists accountability. Harnessing the power of public relations merely suggests that when an HBCU steps forward in research, innovation or service, it should take care to have representatives of the media present to witness and record it (Stewart, 2001). Amid the closing, and near closings of institutions, the experience of matriculating at a historically Black college has been defamed in news reporting by those without an understanding of the nuances of HBCU culture (Stewart, 2001). The hostile social climate heightens the stakes of communicating the intangible treasures that administrators, faculty, current students, and alumni know reside on HBCU campuses. As those with an intimate knowledge of it, the priority of public relations practitioners is to aid key publics in appreciating why HBCUs remain a critical component of the educational landscape in the United States, deserving of broad-based support.

## BIBLIOGRAPHY

Brunner, B. R., and Boyer, L. (2008). Internet presence and historically Black colleges and universities: Protecting their images on the World Wide Web? *Public Relations Review, 34*, 80–82. doi: doi:10.101.1016/j.pubrev.2007.08.020.

Carolina Story: Virtual Museum of University History. (2004). *African Americans and integration.* Retrieved March 11, 2018, from https://museum.unc.edu/exhibits/show/integration/commencement-2004.

Gallup. (2015). *Gallup-USA funds minority college graduates report.* Washington, DC: Gallup World Headquarters.

Gasman, M., and Drezner, N. D. (2009). A Maverick in the field: The Oram group and fundraising in the Black college community during the 1970s. *History of Education Quarterly, 49*(4), 465–500. doi: 10.1111/j.1748-5959.2009.00226.x.

Gasman, M., and Drezner, N. D. (2010). Fundraising for Black colleges during the 1960s and 1970s: The case of hampton institute. *Nonprofit & Voluntary Sector Quarterly, 39*(2), 321–342.

Hill, S. T. (1982). *The traditionally Black institutions of higher education 1860 to 1982* (131). Washington, DC: National Center for Education Statistics.

Luckie, M. S. (October 26, 2015). I went to a Black college because of "a different world." *BuzzFeed.* https://http://www.buzzfeed.com/marksluckie/i-went-to-an-hbcu-because-of-a-different-world?utm_term=.opgPbEY57G - .oiD5AJxQNY.

McCee, Bernard. (2008). *HBCUs – still useful and viable* (Vol. 24, pp. 5–5). Cox Matthews & Associates Inc.

Mcclure, B. (2011). It's a different world! https://stateofhbcus.wordpress.com/2011/05/05/its-a-different-world.

Petrie, P. W. (2007). Alma mater, how we love thee, editorial. *Crisis (15591573),* 2–2. https://elib.uah.edu/login?url=http://search.ebscohost.com/login.aspx?direct=true&db=a9h&AN=34518736&site=ehost-live&scope=site.

Riley, J. L. (2010). Black colleges need a new mission. *Wall Street Journal - Eastern Edition, 256*(75), A21.

Stewart, D. (2001). Advice to HBCUs: Use the media to your advantage. *Black Issues in Higher Education, 18*(13), 31.

Tindall, N. T. J. (2007). Fund-raising models at public historically Black colleges and universities. *Public Relations Review, 33*(2), 201–205. doi: https://doi.org/10.1016/j.pubrev.2007.02.004.

United Negro College Fund, Inc. (2017). *HBCUs make America strong: The positive impact of histoically Black colleges and universities* (8). Washington, DC: United Negro College Fund, Inc.

Wilcox, D., Cameron, G., Ault, P., and Agee, W. (2003). *Public relations strategies and tactics* (7th ed.). Boston: Pearson Education.

*Chapter 6*

# Intercollegiate Athletics

## *Support for Campus Recognition and Financial Exigency*

### Amber Fallucca

## FRAMING HBCU INTERCOLLEGIATE ATHLETICS

Intercollegiate athletics is a major contributor to American higher education, and is increasingly looked to for means of elevating campus identities regardless of institutional size or type. Formalized athletics became visible in higher education starting in 1852 with the rowing event between Harvard and Yale, and has experienced growth ever since (Thelin, 1994; Clotfelter, 2011). Historically Black colleges and universities (HBCUs) began their journey with college athletics through significant events like the first recorded football game between Livingstone College and Biddleton College (now Johnson C. Smith University) in 1892 (Cooper, Cavil, and Cheeks, 2014). Today, collegiate sports support the name recognition of many HBCU institutions, as well as providing financial benefits to these schools through student-athlete participation, thus boosting enrollment and potential tuition support, and alumni and donor giving (Tucker, 2004). While positive outcomes exist, questions emerge about the sustainability of the current HBCU athletics model moving forward, and thus institutional leadership efforts are continually reviewing current strategies. Additionally, the tangible and perceived contributions of intercollegiate athletics will likely influence the organizational structure and resource allotments within the campus community, and thus relationships with institutional leadership and associated priorities are also significant.

## COLLEGE ATHLETICS HISTORY AND INFLUENTIAL DECISIONS

HBCUs joined the intercollegiate athletic movement after early similar beginnings across predominantly White institutions (PWIs), yet they maintain an established and well-regarded history. Specifically, HBCUs can look to the efforts of early pioneers like E. B. Henderson (basketball supporter) and winning teams (e.g., Tennessee State women's track and field teams, Tuskegee football teams) for the continuance of HBCU sport participation and success (Cooper, Cavil, and Cheeks, 2014). The development of HBCUs as initiated through the second Morrill Act (1890) provided the early foundations for which institutions were established and athletics departments could emerge (Redd, 1998*)*. Additionally, organized athletics at HBCUs developed in similar time periods as community-based organizations where individual characteristics including cultural identity and masculinity emerged, thus generating further societal support for college athletics (Cavil, 2015).

Four HBCU athletic conferences were introduced during the years 1912 to 1969, and continue to represent the major athletic conferences across forty-five institutions today (Cheeks, 2016). These conferences were formed and initiated as follows: Colored Intercollegiate Athletic Association—renamed Central Intercollegiate Athletic Conference (CIAA; 1912), Southern Intercollegiate Athletic Conference (SIAC; 1913), Southwestern Athletic Conference (SWAC; 1920), and the Mid-Eastern Athletic Conference (MEAC; 1969) (Gaither, 2013). For HBCUs, regardless of size or reputation, the athletics programs within these aforementioned conferences set the tone and perception of HBCUs across the country. This trend follows what occurs across the landscape of higher education institutions as athletics serves as the "front porch of the institution" (Toma and Cross, 1998), therefore utilizing college sport to emphasize institutional prestige and recognition.

Federal policy generated a different path for HBCUs that greatly influenced the role of athletics programs on these campuses. The trajectory of HBCUs and college athletics was forever altered with the 1954 *Brown v. Board of Education* decision that provided the springboard for integration across higher education institutions. Thus, African American student-athletes initially prohibited from enrolling at PWIs were soon actively recruited to these schools. In response, a competitive market for elite athletic talent emerged, and subsequently HBCUs found themselves challenged in attracting students of similar athletic caliber (Cheeks, 2016). This trend was not isolated to college athletes, and thus many HBCUs struggled to redefine their purpose and identity in order to attract students to maintain current enrollment goals and financial stability (Redd, 1998; Sink, 1995).

Another regulatory consideration involves the National Collegiate Athletics Association (NCAA), officially formed in 1910 to manage athletics reform across the scope of national college athletics programs, and then over time evolved to provide regional and national championships support, distribution of athletics scholarships, and enforcement of player safety policies and administrative regulations (Washington, 2004). Emphases on revenue distribution and brand recognition have advanced HBCU athletics developments (Jones and Bell, 2016). However, implementation of Title IX has created some challenges due to the increased necessity to fund women's sports at similar rates as men's teams. In addition, further emphases on student-athlete well-being and associated resources, including academic support, thus exacerbates an already challenging financial situation for HBCU athletics departments (Smith, 2000; Jolly, 2008). Policy advancements have focused on legislatively supporting HBCUs, including a presidential executive order to help focus energies on HBCU participation across federally sponsored programs ("What is an executive order," n.d.). It is clear that HBCUs and intercollegiate athletics have been greatly influenced by federal regulatory policy decisions.

## CURRENT STATUS OF
## COLLEGE ATHLETICS AT HBCUs

Of the HBCU institutions with varsity athletics programs, twenty-four exist in the most competitive division, NCAA Division I, distributed across two athletics conferences, SWAC and MEAC. The remaining institutions exist at either the NCAA Division II (twenty-nine institutions), Division III level (one institution), NAIA (eighteen institutions), or Community College level (two institutions) (Jones and Bell, 2016). Naturally, financial implications are varied for HBCU institutions situated across these athletic competition categories. Depending upon the college campuses, intercollegiate athletics can be recognized as a major contributor to the visibility of the institution through athletic contests, marketing, and branding efforts, and the ability for athletics to propel an institutional profile forward in unique ways (Fisher, 2009; Jackson, Lyons, and Gooden, 2001). Furthermore, as the interest in sports on college campuses increases, so does the interest by alumni and subsequently, donors to the institution (Stinson and Howard, 2008). Another consistent theme emerges regarding the perceived value of successful athletics programs as continually acknowledged by leadership across varied institutional types and sizes (Frans, 2002). While questions exist, there are important distinctions to consider across HBCU institutions. A direct relationship exists between competitive skill level and financial budget size, and thus institutional implications are likely to emerge based upon the emphasis placed on intercollegiate athletics.

## Division I—"Big Time" Athletics

While not all HBCU institutions fall in the Division 1 category those with football programs especially represent the common public perception of HBCU institutions and athletic programs (McClelland, 2011). With this recognition comes significant pressure to elevate positive characteristics and outcomes that will then filter down to lesser visible HBCU schools. Fewer opportunities have existed for HBCU athletics departments to elevate programs and gain the significant recognition traditionally reserved for PWIs. Therefore, HBCUs often leverage the strategies that do exist; the next section highlights notable successful approaches.

## Guarantee Contract Games

Division I HBCU football and men's basketball teams are sought after and encouraged to play highly competitive PWI teams in a "payout" structure where participation equates to large contributions to the overall athletic department budget (Faure and Cranor, 2010). While these opportunities are continuing to increase and provide a significant source of revenue for HBCU athletics programs (upward of several hundred thousand dollars), there are questions about the viability of these contests since player safety and wellness (e.g., missed class, increased travel) may be at risk (Lillig, 2015). For example, in 2014 Savannah State University earned more than $800,000 for playing three guarantee games in one season with a collective total scoring deficit of −192 points. While the payout supported the institution in significant ways, the accompanying negative influence on morale and perceptions of the school can also lead to unintended outcomes (Lillig, 2015). Positive results are possible as noted by Texas Southern University's basketball win over Michigan State University in 2014 that also generated a $95,000 payout for the winning team (Medcalf, 2014), and thus the pay-for-play model can provide multiple benefits to HBCU participants. However, it should be noted that due to the newer playoff system in place for the most competitive football programs, success is being redefined to measure the quality of opponents beyond expected winning performance outcomes (Lillig, 2009). Therefore, HBCU football programs will likely be vetted more carefully to ensure they fulfill valued criteria before being asked to participate in guarantee games.

Beyond team performance, HBCUs can also utilize the guarantee game to bring awareness of their institutional characteristics. One current successful example involves the efforts of Grambling State to utilize highly marketed games against quality competition to showcase the institution. For example, parades, reunions across graduates, and the traditional battle of the bands help to create an atmosphere supportive of a "great financial windfall" and potential "recruiting tool for not only athletics, but our universities as a whole" (Rodgers, 2015, 157).

## Opportunities for All Institutional Types

Beyond the unique cases afforded to the most competitive HBCU athletics teams, all HBCU institutions share a collective goal to pursue strategies to support the viability of their schools. Examples based upon twenty-first century trends and future-oriented planning across HBCUs are described in the next section.

## Revisit Relationship with Governing Bodies

The NCAA has provided a foundational model for governance of intercollegiate athletics, including the majority of HBCU institutions with athletics programs. While these standards have historically elevated the quality of programs sponsored by the NCAA, evidence supports the need to revisit the impact of such decisions on HBCU athletics programs (Cooper, Cavil, and Cheeks, 2014). HBCUs share a similar unique identity and common institutional characteristics and goals; therefore, it may be helpful to revisit the governance model that aligns best in advancing their distinctive institutional missions. For example, conference-level commitments to member institutions have proven successful when affiliated colleges collectively work together (e.g., television contracts; Cheeks, 2016). Furthermore, the community-based characteristics that many HBCUs emphasize as part of their institutional cultures can also influence larger decisions regarding athletics governance alignment. For example, reviewing geographic regions or traditional rivalries to support increased game attendance and competitive levels for conference membership could lead to positive outcomes (e.g., ticket sales).

Additional governance models could exist to transform HBCU athletics in a large way (e.g., paying players; Hruby, 2017), or minimally be revisited in conjunction with the current NCAA structure emphasizing holistic approaches supporting the student-athlete and college experience (Hosick, 2016). Regardless, an initial step is to involve all HBCU institutions to ensure collective goals are identified to generate a unified approach.

## Recruitment of Diverse Student-Athlete Populations

Another continuing trend across HBCUs includes the increasing number of student-athletes not identifying as African American, thus creating a growing diverse student population and conditions for tuition-paying opportunities due to the desire for some students to continue a potentially stymied athletics career into college (Jones and Bell, 2016). This trend follows overall HBCU enrollment patterns as increasingly number of student enrollees at HBCUS identify themselves other than African American (Gasman, 2013; Greenlee, 2001; Oguntoyinbo, 2015). Furthermore, international students participating in intercollegiate athletics can provide teams with desirable athletics skills while also demonstrating satisfaction with the institution they are attending (Trendafilova, Hardin, and Kim, 2010). Another consideration for HBCUs is to consider the impact of Pell Grant and other non-athletics scholarship-based awards on the characteristics of student-athletes being recruited. For example, federal or other external funding can help increase student-athlete enrollment as well as support institutional tuition and financial goals (Perna et al., 2008).

## Elevate Community Connections and Alumni Support

HBCU Classic Football Games typically occur between two notable rivals, yet more significantly they also serve as a prominent tradition to help bring alumni, donors, and broader communities together (Suggs, 2000; Stone, Cort, and Nkonge, 2012). Such annual events can emerge in different forms but common characteristics include the marquee game during the typical college football season and additional events beyond the game, typically spanning a three-day period of social events and networking opportunities (Rodgers, 2015; Seymour, 2006). African American attendees' economic spending during Classic Games increases based upon factors related to loyalty and sport-related behaviors (Armstrong, 2002). These findings suggest that HBCUs have a promising opportunity to capitalize on tradition-based sporting events, such as football Classic games or potentially developed across other competitive sports, to connect with interested community members and associated potential donors. Furthermore, as new generations of fans emerge, HBCUs could benefit by revisiting Classic Game traditions to ensure associated activities appeal to younger attendees, thus increasing potential loyalty and giving behaviors.

## Institutional Support for Athletics Programs

There appears to be little question that when done well, athletics and academics can work in harmony to elevate an institutional profile. For example, the Air Force Reserve Celebration football bowl game occurs every year and posits the winning teams from the two Division I conferences comprised of HBCU institutions to play in this nationally televised game. While difficult to quantify, both schools receive increased visibility and confidence to their viability due to participation in the high-profile game in similar ways that PWI schools have achieved (Humphreys and Mondello, 2007). Additionally, institutions that grow in enrollment over time can also naturally increase the number of potential alumni and donors, thus leading to a positive effect on institutional endowments. For example, Bethune-Cookman almost doubled endowment across the span of four years, and such capacity to build endowments exists and athletics can be one vehicle to support these efforts (Gill and Hart, 2015). Furthermore, support for student-athletes during their collegiate years can also provide a later benefit when professional sport or other industry-based achievements can lead to increased athlete participant giving back to his/her alma mater (O'Neil and Schenke, 2007).

An important consideration for HBCUs regards institutional strategic planning and ensuring that athletics programs remain solvent to therefore boost institutional confidence and support. One current trend is the use of student funds to subsidize college athletics as many HBCU institutions do so at a rate of 50 percent or higher (Cheeks, 2016). Such financial decisions are not unique to HBCU schools and are adapted by many institutional types. While currently considered a sustainable method, this trend may not be realistic to continue due to additional financial pressures (Cheeks and Carter-Francique, 2015; Ridpath, 2014).

## Revisit Sport Programs Offering and Potential for Change

Athletics departments and the number of affiliated sport programs will differ by school, and thus institutions would benefit from thinking strategically about how athletics sport offerings complement institutional goals and mission. The most common sports sponsored by HBCUs include basketball (men and women) followed by track and field, football (men only) baseball/softball, tennis and volleyball (women only) (Jones and Bell, 2016). While tennis is still popular, this sport and golf have also experienced the most decrease in sport offerings across HBCU institutions. Key questions institutions should consider for each sport include operating budget size required, facilities development and maintenance, and demand across participant and audience interest, including the opportunities for corporate sponsorships (apparel, televised events, ticket sales; Harrington, and Johnson, 2014) to support the longitudinal goals of the athletics program and also athletics department and institution. In addition, it might be beneficial to revisit the athletics scholarship structure by HBCU schools. NCAA Division III schools are unable to provide athletics-based aid, however student-athletes can qualify for need-based, academic, or other types of scholarship funding. Conversely, institutions from the National Association of Intercollegiate Athletics (NAIA) can provide athletics-based scholarships, therefore encouraging coaches and athletics departments to recruit student-athletes utilizing athletics-based resources (e.g., recruiting budgets, scholarship packages).

## STUDENT-ATHLETE PARTICIPANT OUTCOMES

Regardless of institutional size, much evidence exists to support the participatory benefits of college students engaging in intercollegiate athletics. It should be noted the extensive competitive environment existing for participants wanting to play collegiate sport. For example, in 2016 approximately 8 million kids played high school sports, a new all-time high. Of these, 170,000 (close to 2 percent) received a sports scholarship across all institutional types (NCAA, n.d.). Those few athletes who make it to the HBCU college ranks, positive outcomes exist relating to personal and academic success (Brown, 2004; Cooper and Hawkins, 2012).

Comparative to non-HBCU schools, positive gains are noted in the areas of identity development beyond athletics and opportunities for campus engagement for HBCU student-athletes (Jones and Bell, 2016). These findings suggest HBCU student-athletes can experience a more holistic college experience, beyond the narrow confines of successful sport participation. Tangible examples that may set HBCU athletics experiences apart from non-HBCU institutions include opportunities for smaller class sizes, positive connections with professors, and increased academic support (Cooper and Hawkins, 2012; Cooper, 2018; New, 2015). Another positive evidence point is related to life after sport outcomes. The NCAA currently collects this information through student-athlete exit surveys. A common challenge across all higher education institutions is to study the successful students after they graduate due to lacking communication and comprehensive tracking of next destinations (Cohen, 2006). HBCU institutions are likely to have informed connections with alumni based upon the community events and increased networking opportunities (Gasman, 2001). Given this premise and the tangible transferable skills procured through college athletics participation, such connections can help elevate athletics experiences and subsequent professional and personal successes to showcase the benefits of the athlete experience. Evidence does exist demonstrating positive outcomes for college athletics participation, specific to HBCUs and across all institutional types (Gawrysiak, Cooper, and Hawkins, 2013; Gayles and Hu, 2009).

### Activity

Given the promising outcomes for HBCU student-athletes, as well as the identified encouraging practices that exist for related college athletics departments to support their institutional missions and enrollment and financial goals, HBCUs should make several considerations to maximize the athletics roles at these institutions. The activity and prompts are intended to advance institutional thinking with regard to the role of college athletics within the context of HBCUs and strategic planning (see table 6.1). For example, institutions at the most competitive level of sport classification (Division I) should consider how best to balance the opportunity to play PWI opponents in a "pay-for-play" structure when travel, potential injury, and player/program confidence can be negatively impacted. Furthermore, institutions should consider how to leverage marketing opportunities associated with such major games, and utilize the influence HBCU institutions hold at this highly competitive level to ensure they are maximizing opportunities through the identified governing body (e.g., NCAA).

The section entitled "All Divisions" provides strategic questions for leadership to consider applicable across all institutional types. Specifically, how are institutions looking to intercollegiate athletics programs to meet strategic

**Table 6.1   Considerations for HBCU Leadership with Regards to Athletics Department Decision Making**

Division I
*Opportunities for pay-for-play games specific to football and basketball*
- What is the balance between funding opportunities through athletic contests and student-athlete well-being?
- What are the ways to capitalize on marketing opportunities based upon new audiences and exposure?
- What are the athletics department/institutional goals relative to the current governing body (e.g., NCAA)?

All Divisions
*Recruitment of diverse athletes to college sport teams*
- What are the ways institutions can attract and recruit competitive athletes to play for HBCUs?
  - Emphasis on providing overall support for student-athletes (academic, nutrition, facilities)

*Elevate community connections and alumni support through athletics events*
- What are the ways that coaches and student-athletes can visibly contribute to the community?
- How can former players and teams be included as part of alumni initiatives?
  - Utilize sporting events as community gathering place
  - Identify former student-athletes for alumni giving purposes

*Revisit how institutions practically and symbolically support athletics programs*
- How does the institutional leadership promote the athletics programs?
- What role do faculty have with intercollegiate programs?
- How do institutions support student-athletes beyond the playing field? Internship placement? Career readiness?

*Revisit sport programs offerings to ensure they align with institutional goals*
- Are teams continually vetted for continued interest/popularity by athletes and audiences and balanced financial budgets?

goals related to enrollment growth and diverse student populations? Further-more, HBCUs should consider how athletics events and alumni and donor initiatives are connected. Promising practices exist to ensure athletics games and associated events elicit increased loyalty. Lastly, institutions should also emphasize the relative untapped resource of student-athletes graduates, a group whose later professional success (and potential donor giving behaviors) may be greatly influenced by on-field and holistic campus-oriented experiences.

## CONCLUSION

In conclusion, as HBCUs continue to define and defend their unique roles within the higher education landscape, a promising strategy focuses on supporting the excitement and energy surrounding intercollegiate athletics. This chapter described the history of intercollegiate athletics across HBCUs, and methods for how athletics' presence on the college campus can increase an institution's visibility through alumni support and associated giving, as well as by creating an environment for positive long-term outcomes for its athletic participants. Additional examples focused on related revenue streams (e.g., payout games and tuition-paying student-athletes) as means for college sports to provide value to institutions' financial exigency. Furthermore, as demonstrated through the provided activity (table 6.1), key questions guiding athletics decision-making can be applied across a variety of institutional types. One notable example includes the significance of unity across HBCU institutions to influence current and ideal governance structures, and thus helps to ensure institutions' collective goals are being met. These emphases can help maximize financial stability of HBCUs, thus preserving the traditions and quality of student experiences to ensure strong viable futures for these institutions.

## BIBLIOGRAPHY

Armstrong, K. L. (2002). An examination of the social psychology of Blacks' consumption of sport. *Journal of Sport Management, 16*(4), 267–288.

Brown, J. M. (2004). *Perceptions and performance of African American male student-athletes at a historically Black university and a predominantly white university (Doctoral Dissertation).* Retrieved from http://repository.lib.ncsu.edu/ir/bitstream/1840.16/3751/1/etd.pdf.

Cavil, J. K. (2015). Early athletic experiences at HBCUs: The creation of conferences. In B. Hawkins, J. Cooper, A. Carter-Francique, and J. K. Cavil (Eds.), *The athletic experience at historically Black colleges and universities: Past, present, and persistence* (19–57). Lanham, MD: Rowman & Littlefield.

Cheeks, G. (2016). *A critical examination of NCAA Division I HBCU athletic director's perspective of the current state of intercollegiate athletics (Doctoral dissertation).* Proquest Dissertations and Theses database. (No. 10290910).

Cheeks, G., and Carter-Francique, A. R. (2015). HBCUs versus HWCUs: A critical examination of institutional distancing between collegiate athletic programs. *Race, Gender, & Class, 22*(1), 23–35.

Clotfelter, C. T. (2011). *Big-time sports in American universities.* New York: Cambridge University Press.

Cohen, R. T. (2006). Black college alumni giving: A study of the perceptions, attitudes, and giving behaviors of alumni donors at selected historically Black colleges and universities. *International Journal of Educational Advancement, 6*(3), 200–220.

Cooper, J. N. (2018). Strategic navigation: A comparative study of Black male scholar athletes' experiences at a Historically Black College/University (HBCU) and Historically White University (HWU). *International Journal of Qualitative Studies in Education, 31*(4), 235–256.

Cooper, J. N., Cavil, J. K., and Cheeks, G. (2014). The state of intercollegiate athletics at historically Black colleges and universities (HBCUs): Past, present, and persistence. *Journal of Issues in Intercollegiate Athletics, 7,* 307–332.

Cooper, J. N., and Hawkins, B. (2012). A place of opportunity: Black male student athletes' experiences at a historically Black university. *Journal of Intercollegiate Sport, 5*(2), 170–188.

Faure, C. E., and Cranor, C. (2010). Pay for slay: An examination of the repercussions of the big money game on the little guy in college football. *Journal of Issues in Intercollegiate Athletics, 2010,* 194–210.

Fisher, B. (2009). Athletics success and institutional rankings. *New Directions for Higher Education, 148,* 45–53.

Frans, K. A. (2002). *Ways in which intercollegiate athletics contribute to university success* (Unpublished master's thesis). North Carolina State University, Raleigh, NC.

Gaither, S. J. (January 2013). Despite great strides, HBCUs and NCA-recognized athletic conferences face challenges. *Diverse Issues in Higher Education.* http://diverseeducation.com/article/50844.

Gasman, M. (2013). *The changing face of historically Black colleges and universities.* Center for Minority Serving Institutions, University of Pennsylvania, Philadelphia.

Gasman, M. (2001). An untapped resource: Bringing African Americans into the college and university giving process. *The CASE International Journal of Educational Advancement, 2*(3), 280–292.

Gawrysiak, E. J., Cooper, J. N., and Hawkins, B. (2013). The impact of baseball participation on the educational experiences of Black student-athletes at historically Black colleges and universities. *Race Ethnicity and Education, 18*(5), 1–27. doi: 10.1080/13613324.2013.792795.

Gayles, J. G., and Hu, S. (2009). The influence of student engagement and sport participation on college outcomes among division I student athletes. *The Journal of Higher Education, 80*(3), 315–333.

Gill, E., and Hart, A. (2015). Separate, unequal, and irrelevant. In B. Hawkins, J. Cooper, A. Carter-Francique, and J. Cavil (Eds.), *The athletic experience at historically Black colleges and universities: Past, present, and persistence* (181–203). Lanham, MD: Rowman & Littlefield.

Greenlee, C. T. (2001). Bowled over by women competitors. *Black Issues in Higher Education, 18*(8), 90–91.

Harrington, C. F., and Johnson, G. D. (2014). Customer relationship management and intercollegiate athletics: Opportunities and benefits for smaller institutions. *Management and Organizational Studies, 1*(1), 1–6.

Hosick, M. B. (April 1, 2016). *HBCUs, limited resource schools to benefit from initiatives.* http://www.ncaa.org/about/resources/media-center/news/hbcus-limited-resource-schools-benefit-initiatives.

Hruby, P. (July 20, 2017). *The plot to disrupt the NCAA with a pay-for-play HBCU basketball league.* https://sports.vice.com/en_us/article/59zejz/the-plot-to-disrupt-the-ncaa-with-a-pay-for-play-hbcu-basketball-league.

Humphreys, B. R., and Mondello, M. (2007). Intercollegiate athletic success and donations at NCAA division I institutions. *Journal of Sport Management, 21*(2), 265–280.

Jackson, E. N., Lyons, R., and Gooden, S. C. (2001). The marketing of Black college sports. *Sport Marketing Quarterly, 10*, 138–146.

Jolly, J. C. (2008). Raising the question #9: Is the student-athlete population unique? And why should we care? *Communication Education, 57*(1), 145–151.

Jones, W. A., and Bell, L. F. (2016). Status report on HBCU athletics: Participation, finances, and student experiences. *Journal for the Study of Sports and Athletes in Education, 10*(1), 48–74.

Lillig, J. C. (2009). Magic or misery: HBCUs, guarantee contracts, and public policy. *Journal of Sports Law and Contemporary Problems, 6*(41), 41–72.

Lillig, J. C. (2015). Financing HBCU athletics: Men's basketball-problems and opportunities. In B. Hawkins, J. Cooper, A. Carter-Francique, and J. K. Cavil (Eds.), *The athletic experience at historically Black colleges and universities* (207–227). Lanham, MD: Rowman & Littlefield.

McClelland, C. F. (2011). *Athletic directors' perceptions of the effectiveness of HBCU division I-AA athletics programs (Doctoral dissertation).* Dissertation Abstracts International database (No. 885653989).

Medcalf, Myron. (December 30, 2014). Shocker: Michigan state loses to Texas southern. *ESPN.com.* http://www.espn.com/blog/collegebasketballnation/post/_/id/10161l/shocker-texas-southern-wins-at-michigan-state.

National Collegiate Athletics Association (NCAA). (n.d.). *Scholarships.* https://www.ncaa.org/student-athletes/future/scholarships (accessed July 21, 2017).

New, J. (October 28, 2015). *Positive news for HBCUs.* https://www.insidehighered.com/news/2015/10/28/survey-finds-big-differences-between-black-hbcu-graduates-those-who-attended-other.

Oguntoyinbo, L. (September 29, 2015). The influx of Latinos at historically Black colleges. *The Atlantic.* https://www.theatlantic.com/education/archive/2015/09/hbcus-more-latino-students/407953.

O'Neil, J., and Schenke, M. (2007). An examination of factors impacting athlete alumni donations to their alma mater: A case study of a U.S. university. *International Journal of Nonprofit and Volunteer Sector Marketing, 12*(1), 59–74.

Perna, L. W., Rown-Kenyon, H., Bell, A., Thomas, S. L., and Li, C. (2008). A typology of federal and state programs designed to promote college enrollment. *The Journal of Higher Education, 79*(3), 243–267.

Redd, K. E. (1998). Historically Black colleges and universities: Making a comeback. *New Directions for Higher Education, 102*, 33–43.

Ridpath, D. (December 12, 2014). *How we're secretly funding college athletic programs.* http://www.thefiscaltimes.com/2014/12/12/How-We-re-Secretly-Funding-College-Athletic-Programs.

Rodgers, R. P. (2015). "It's HBCU classic time!": Origins and the perseverance of historically Black college and university football classic games. In B. Hawkins, J. Cooper, A. Carter-Francique, and J. Cavil (Eds.), *The athletic experience at historically Black colleges and universities: Past, present, and persistence* (145–165). Lanham, MD: Rowman & Littlefield.

Seymour, A. (2006). Pigskin payday. *Diverse Issues in Higher Education, 23*(23), 36–39.

Sink, J. D. (1995). Public policy and America's land-grant educational enterprise: The unique West Virginia experience. *Journal of Negro Education, 64*(1), 6–14.

Smith, R. K. (2000). A brief history of the national collegiate athletic association's role of regulating intercollegiate athletics. *Marquette Sports Law Review, 11*(9), 9–22.

Stinson, J. L., and Howard, D. R. (2008). Winning does matter: Patterns in private giving to athletic and academic programs at NCAA division I-AA and I-AAA institutions. *Sport Management Review, 11*(1), 1–20.

Stone, G. W., Cort, K. T., and Nkonge, J. (2012). An exploratory model of the antecedent factors contributing to fan support/attendance at HBCU basketball games. *Atlantic Marketing Journal, 1*(1), 15–30.

Suggs, W. (October 20, 2000). For Black Americans, better than a bowl game. *Chronicle of Higher Education, 47*(8), A52–A53.

Thelin, J. R. (1994). *Games colleges play: Scandal and reform in intercollegiate athletics.* Baltimore: John Hopkins University Press.

Trendafilova, S., Hardin, R., and Kim, S. (2010). Satisfaction among international student-athletes who participate in the national collegiate athletic association. *Journal of Intercollegiate Sport, 3*(2), 348–365.

Toma, J. D., and Cross, M. (1998). Intercollegiate athletics and student college choice: Exploring the impact of championship seasons on undergraduate applications. *Research in Higher Education, 39*, 633–661.

Tucker, I. B. (2004). A reexamination of the effect of big-time football and basketball success on graduation rates and alumni giving rates. *Economics of Education, 23*(5), 655–661.

Washington, M. (2004). Field approaches to institutional change: The evolution of the national collegiate athletic association 1906–1995. *Organization Studies, 25*(3), 393–414.

"What is an executive order" (n.d.). https://tmcf.org/our-policy/executive-orders.

*Chapter 7*

# On the Road to Success

## *The Beneficialness of African American Women's Leadership at HBCU's*

### LaShanda Y. Hague

## LITERATURE REVIEW

### History of African American Academic Leadership

African American women have been leading in college and university presidency positions since the beginning of the nineteenth century (Coleman, 2012; Gaston, 2015). The lineage of African American women presidents began in 1904 when Mary McLeod Bethune found Daytona Normal and Industrial Institute for Negro Girls in Daytona, Florida. During her twenty-year presidency, the school experienced growth from five students to over two hundred and fifty (Gaston, 2015). Of course, there have been other prominent female presidents including Johnetta Besch Cole (Spelman College), Julianne Malveaux (Bennett College), Dorothy Yancy (Johnson C. Smith), and Carolyn Meyers (Jackson State University) (Gasman and Commodore, 2014).

Historically research shows that African American women have been participants in higher education for more than 100 years, but rarely was the impact of racism and sexism on African American women in academia examined (Moses, 1989). Studies that examined the experiences of African American women administrators on predominantly White campuses were limited. The focal point of many studies and surveys conducted on Blacks in higher education was on Black males. African Americans confronted obstacles on what they could be and accomplish, as well as experienced harsh treatments in educational institutions and had to develop unconventional ways to advocate for themselves and those in the community (Moses, 1989).

Henry (as cited in Montgomery and Bradford, 2010) indicates African American women college/university presidents expand the criterion of higher education, encourage countless students and colleagues, and heighten the standards of learning at universities across the country. They are champions and trailblazers in higher education during a time when race and gender are still too often regarded as challenges. Specifically, in the twenty-first century, African American women have learned the crucial importance of earning a degree in higher education in the context of their current struggles. Nevertheless, African American women who aspire to advance in mid-level up to executive-level leadership positions in higher education face many barriers and challenges (Montgomery and Bradford, 2010).

## Critical Race Theory and Black Feminist Theory

Critical race theory hypothesizes that race and racism are the main principles in understanding the ways in which theory, policy, and practice are used to lessen African American people, while upholding White supremacy in the United States (Solorzano, 1997; 1998). Gaetane, Williams, and Sherman (2009) utilized critical race theory in their study to explain the experiences of African American women leaders in higher education and examine the intersectionality of race and gender. Black women's Afrocentric ways of knowing emerges from the richness of their African roots, which inform what they believe to be true about themselves and their experiences. Black women draw from common experiences that historically connect them to the fundamental elements of an Afrocentric epistemology (i.e., oppression resulting from colonialism, slavery, apartheid, imperialism, and other systems of racial domination) (Collins, 1996, 2000; McLean and Johansen, 2006).

Black feminist theory centralizes and validates the intersecting dimensions of race and gender that are uniquely experienced in the lives of African American women. It is grounded on the assumption that the majority of Black women share commonalities, perceptions, and experiences (Henry and Glenn, 2009). Black women perceive more obstacles to and receive less assistance with their advancement in organizations in which they have worked (Key, Popkin, Munchus, Wech, Hill, and Tanner, 2012).

## Structural Perspective of Leadership

The structural perspective proposes the nature of organizational structures and the organization of work rather than individuals or gender roles. One's position on the impact of organizational structure on the career advancement of women is based on the belief that the individual forms the organization or the organization forms the individual (Timmers, Willemsen, and Tjidens, 2010).

The continued selection of African American women as presidents are notable and indicate a possible shift in the way HBCU boards are selecting presidents. The most recent selections are serving at a time many consider the pinnacle of awareness of HBCU leadership and administrative practices (Gasman, M. and Commodore, 2014). As we consider their success, what can help African American women to overcome obstacles in their paths that hinder advancement to top-level administration? Montgomery and Bradford (2010) acknowledge important strategies that HBCUs should consider:

- Promoting participation of African American women at all levels of the university's infrastructure.
- Engaging in conversations critical to the success and advancement of African American women in higher education.
- Eradicating "insider trading" so African American women are not unjustly excluded from the pool of qualified candidates for senior administrative positions.
- Creating networking opportunities that promote interaction with current and former African American women administrators (see figures 7.1 and 7.2).

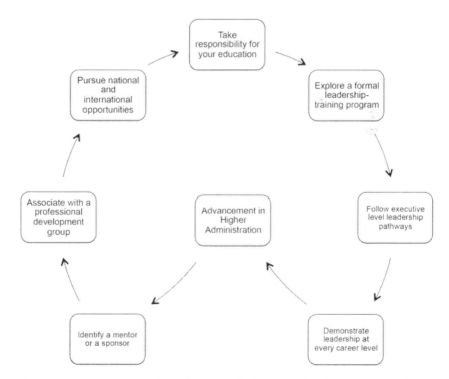

**Figure 7.1   Model for effective advancement of African American women in higher administration at HBCUs.**

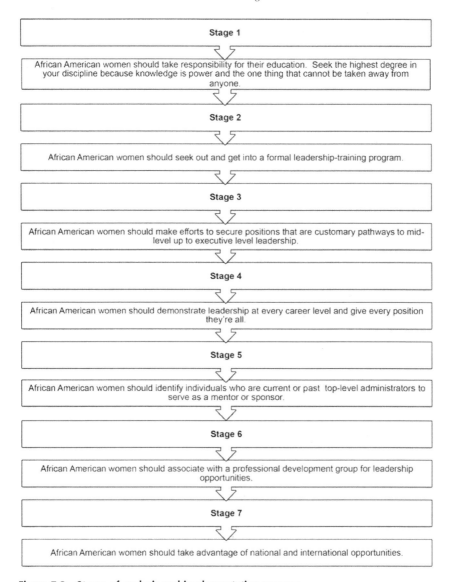

Figure 7.2    Stages of analysis and implementation process.


## RECOMMENDATIONS

The following recommendations for HBCUs address how advancing African American women aspiring to be in leadership will benefit them. HBCUs have long depended on students, faculty members, and administrators who place foremost importance on the value of their mission. HBCUs are strengthened by strengthening the pipeline of administrators that run them (Gardner, 2016). Increasing the number of African American women leaders is important for reasons beyond political correctness. As HBCUs become more diverse and globally connected, more creative and diverse types of leadership will continue to be required (Sanchez-Hucles and Davis, 2010). Targeted recruitment as well as the provision of professional development opportunities for African American women aspiring to be in leadership at HBCUs aid in creating the necessary measures to ensure they are well equipped while in the pipeline (Commodore, Freeman, Gasman, and Carter, 2016).

HBCUs must prepare African American women in various areas through professional development that would aid in not only reaching the HBCU presidency or other leadership positions, but also being successful in the role. HBCUs current presidents can use mentoring and shadowing opportunities to introduce aspiring African American women to interactions with board members as well as faculty. It would be most beneficial to have mentors who are familiar with HBCU culture and shared practices, both explicit and implicit. HBCUs need to provide environments and resources to give nonfaculty members the opportunity to pursue terminal degrees (Commodore, Freeman, Gasman, and Carter, 2016).

## CONCLUSION

Despite the odds, African American women are redefining the college/university presidency and inspiring the next generation of leaders in the academy (Gaston, 2015). Educational scholars must continue to research African American women in higher education leadership in HBCUs. Studies are currently limited, and despite developments in the field, race continues to remain separate from the mainstream discourse of institutional leadership, which only serves to promote the normalizations of whiteness (Ospina and Foldly, 2009). Since research on the impact of race and gender on the career advancement of African American women in higher education leadership at HBCUs is understudied, this chapter provides a framework for understanding their experiences.

## REFERENCES

Byrd, M. Y. (2009a). Telling our stories of leadership: If we don't tell them they won't be told. *Advances in Developing Human Resources, 11*(5), 582–605.

Coleman, M. (2012). Leadership and diversity. *Educational Management Administration & Leadership, 40*(5), 592–609.

Collins, P. H. (1996). The social construction of Black feminist thought. In A. Garry and M. Pearsall (Eds.), *Women, knowledge and reality: Explorations in feminist philosophy.* New York, NY: Routledge, 222–248.

Collins, P. H. (2000). *Black feminist thought: Knowledge, consciousness, and the politics of empowerment.* New York: Routledge, 1–326.

Commodore, F., Freeman, S., Gasman, M., and Carter, C. (2016). "How it's done": The role of mentoring and advice in preparing the next generation of historically Black college and university presidents. *Education Sciences, 6*(19), 1–14.

Davis, D., and Maldonado, C. (2015). Shattering the glass ceiling: The leadership development of African American women in higher education. *Advancing Women in Leadership, 35,* 48–64.

Gaetane, J., Williams, V. A., and Sherman, S. L. (2009). Black women's leadership experiences: Examining the intersectionality of race and gender. *Advances in Developing Human Resources, 11*(5), 562–581.

Gardner, L. (2016). Retired HBCU presidents start search firm for Black-college leaders. *The Chronicle of Higher Education, 62*(26), 1–4.

Gasman, M., and Commodore, F. (2014). *The female Black college president.* https://hbculifestyle.com/female-black-college-president/

Gaston, A. (2015). *For Harriet: A celebration of African American women college presidents.* http://www.forharriet.com/2015/02/a-celebration-of-african-american-women.html#axzz48XsV2F5U

Henry, W., and Glenn, N. (2009). Black women employed in the ivory tower: Connecting for success. *Advancing Women in Leadership, 27*(2), 1–18.

Jean-Marie, G., James, C., and Bynum, S. (2006). Black women activists, leaders, and educators: Transforming urban educational practice. In J. L. Kincheloe, K. Hayes, K. Rose, and P. M. Anderson (Eds.), *The Praeger handbook of urban education* (59–70). Westport, CT: Greenwood.

Key, S., Popkin, S., Munchus, G., Wech, B., Hill, V., and Tanner, J. (2012). An exploration of leadership experiences among white women and women of color. *Journal of Organizational Change Management, 25*(3), 392–404.

McLean, G. N., and Johansen, B. P. (Eds.). (2006). Worldviews of adult learning in the workplace. *Advances in Developing Human Resources, 8*(3), 321–328.

Montgomery, S. L., and Bradford, A. B. (2010). African American women overcome campus obstacles. *Women in Higher Education, 19*(9), 24–25. doi: 10.1002/whe.10097.

Moses, Y. T. (1989). *Black women in academe issues and strategies.* Washington, DC: Project on the Status and Education of Women, Association of American Colleges, 1–28.

Ospina, S., and Foldy, E. G. (2009). A critical review of race and ethnicity in the leadership literature: Surfacing context, power and the collective dimensions of leadership. *Leadership Quarterly, 20,* 876–896. doi: 10.1016/j.leaqua.2009.09.005.

Sanchez-Hucles, J., and Davis, D. (2010). Women and women of color in leadership: Complexity, Identity, and Intersectionality. *American Psychologist, 65*(30), 171–181.

Solorzano, D. (1997). Images and words that wound: Critical race theory, racial stereotyping, and teacher education. *Teacher Education Quarterly, 24*(3), 5–19.

Solorzano, D. (1998). Critical race theory, racial and gender microaggressions, and the experiences of Chicana and Chicano scholars. *International Journal of Qualitative Studies in Education, 11*(1), 121–136.

Timmers, T. M., Willemsen, T. M., and Tijdens, K. G. (2010). Gender diversity policies in universities: A multi-perspective framework of policy measures. *Higher Education, 59*(6), 719–735.

*Chapter 8*

# Life beyond Borders

## *The Importance of Study Abroad Experiences of Students at HBCUs*

### William Pruitt III

Globalization and internationalization strengthens our ability to connect and interact with people in various countries. The demand for international familiarity as it pertains to communication and conducting day-to-day business is becoming a non-negotiable qualification for a number of employment opportunities in the modern economy. As an example, more than sixty-five federal agencies including divergent organizations from the Central Intelligence Agency to the Peace Corps annually seek to fill more than 34,000 positions requiring foreign language skills. These needs are regularly unmet (*Global competence & national needs*, 2005). Learning how to interact and communicate with individuals from all over the world is a skill that most students will need to be successful in their professional and personal lives. These skills can be attained and developed through study abroad participation. However, when looking at study abroad programming as a means to attain those skills, Black students are not represented in high numbers.

## BARRIERS TO STUDY ABROAD

A number of research studies surrounding race and ethnicity have revealed disparities among Black and White students when it comes to studying abroad. During the 2015–2016 academic school year, Black students made up approximately 5.9 percent of America's study abroad population (Institute of International Education). With higher education being tasked with the responsibility of increasing the global competency of tomorrow's workforce, the value of international experiences cannot be overstated. There are barriers to accessibility with study abroad. The barriers for Black students are different from those of their counterparts.

There have been several reasons given as to what causes such low study abroad participation rates among Black students. Some studies assert that few Black students have previous travel experience, and they do not come from well-traveled families. There has been conflicting research as to whether or not previous travel experience influences study abroad participation. However, being introduced to the thought or idea of foreign travel at a young age could at least create some interest and exposure to international opportunities. Familial support is very influential in the decision-making process of most college students, whether it is institutional choice, academic major, curricular activities, or studying abroad.

Other research pertaining to low participation rates states that Black students prioritize employment and desire to enter the workforce as quickly as possible. The opportunity cost associated with studying abroad for Black students could also be a reflection of low participation. Data from 2016 showed that 45 percent of full-time Black college students were also in the labor force (Bureau of Labor Statistics, 2018). Foregoing income and risking losing employment as a result of being abroad for weeks or months can negatively impact the decision to study abroad. Also, it is unrealistic to deny that there are instances when studying abroad has delayed graduation for students. A number of Black students do not want to incur the expense of paying for an additional semester of college. *However, with a well-structured study abroad advising operation and proper planning graduation does not have to be delayed.* It is imperative to begin discussing and preparing for study abroad during student's first or second year of college.

Racial disparities in study abroad can also be attributed to a lack of support from faculty and staff. A single institution study conducted by Holly Carter suggested that faculty and staff members often assume that African American students are not qualified to study abroad or even have an interest in doing so, therefore they do not actively recruit Black students (Carter, 1991). Furthermore, some faculty and staff may not see the importance of studying abroad for students who are already facing financial and academic challenges in the United States higher education system; the assumption is that Black students face these challenges.

The targeted marketing and recruitment efforts of faculty and staff are coupled with the promotional materials used in study abroad advertisements. Black students do not see or hear from students who look like them, and come from similar backgrounds. As a result of this, Black students are unable to picture themselves as participants in study abroad programs. This perpetuates the notion that study abroad is for wealthy, White students, and not Black students.

There is a lengthy list of barriers that restrict accessibility to study abroad opportunities for Black students. The affordability barrier is usually the primary hurdle that is identified as the reason Black students do not study abroad. Studying abroad requires costs that are not typically part of normal tuition and fee structure. An example of these costs include passports, visas, program fees, and airfare. Lending practices surrounding federal and state student loans have expanded to make the transfer of finances more seamless between American and foreign universities. There are also external scholarships that are geared toward students with high financial need.

## Advising

The importance of the academic advising processes as it pertains to the introduction of study abroad opportunities cannot be overstated. University advisors generally serve as the doorway to higher education's academic corridor. Academic advisors can assist students with decision such as declaring an academic major, course selection, and rate of academic progress. The relationship between a student and their academic advisor is one that requires a healthy amount of trust. Therefore, it is vital that advisors indicate the importance of developing their advisee's global competency over the course of their college career.

Understandably, study abroad is not for every student. For those students who display no interest in studying abroad, it is still important that there is a global component to their curriculum. It is important that advisors are able to articulate the importance of global competency to Black students. Explaining how global competency will benefit them in their professional and social experiences may push them to take an interest in becoming global citizens. The private and public sector are avidly seeking more globalized citizens. For example, more than sixty-five federal agencies including divergent organizations from the Federal Bureau of Investigations to the Peace Corp annually seek to fill over 34,000 positions that require foreign language skills. The needs associated with these positions are regularly unmet. Being more globally competent can better position students for the job market upon graduation. The undergraduate curriculum for degree competition can be rigid, but advisors should encourage students to take courses that offer components of diversity and societal awareness (African American studies or International Business). There are also courses that may encourage study abroad participation such as the African American Diaspora, Hispanic studies.

It is important that study abroad is mentioned and considered as early as possible in a student's academic career. The general rule of thumb would be six to twelve months of preparation for a study abroad experience. This should be discussed during first semester advising appointments, first year experience courses, and freshman orientation. The sooner students hear about the opportunities that their university is offering, the more prepared they will be to take advantage of those opportunities.

A recent initiative instituted by the study abroad operation at a university in South Carolina was to hold an annual advisor's conference. The study abroad office hosts a four-hour conference for all advisors throughout the university. At this conference, advisors learn about the different types of study abroad programs, the international partnerships that the university has initiated, and opportunities for advisor can take advantage of to get more involved in campus internationalization efforts.

The reason it was necessary to discuss the more prominent barriers in study abroad participation for Black students in the previous section is because advisors (study abroad and academic) must be prepared to help students navigate those barriers during the advising process. Black students may express sentiments like "I don't have the time to study abroad"; "My family would not approve"; "I have to work"; "I can't afford to study abroad." As advisors it is always good to have tools at your disposal to help students hurdle these legitimate concerns.

When students say that they do not have the time to study abroad, I have always found it helpful to introduce short-term programs. Short-term programs (though not as immersive) are generally held over the break periods (spring break, winter break, summer). The thought of being away for one to six weeks versus an entire semester or year may help lessen student's anxiety. For Black students who express concerns about affordability, it may be helpful to refer to programs in less traditional study abroad regions. For example, the cost of tuition and room and board fees at the University of Ghana add up to approximately $2,000 a semester, which is noticeably less than most in-state tuition rates in the United States. Similar pricing can be found at universities in countries such as Thailand, Haiti, and Jamaica. Outside of the academic expenses, the cost of living is generally lower in these regions, allowing for more affordable extracurricular activities. Extracurricular activities such as domestic travel and cultural excursions add to the intrigue of studying abroad.

## Recruitment

One of the biggest challenges facing study abroad administrators is increasing participation numbers. A frequent question among study abroad professionals is "how many students does your university send on study abroad programs each year?" The answer to this question seems to be indicative of prestige, how effective a study abroad operation is, and the level of priority that is placed on study abroad by university governance. With increased interest in the number of students with study abroad experience, institutions are poised to benefit from an increased focus on student participation in study abroad programs as well.

Due to the myths and challenges surrounding study abroad participation, recruiting Black students to participate in international experiences requires a different approach. Though there is no data that draws a direct correlation, a few researchers have asserted that students of color have few visible examples of successful study abroad role models, and this creates the impression that study abroad is not for them. It is important to express to Black students that study abroad, though infrequent, is not new to the Black community. Many Black activists and celebrities have studied abroad, individuals such as James Meredith, Shirley Chisolm, Russell Hornsby, Holly Robinson Peete, and many more. In addition to studying abroad, many Black Americans have taken an interest in international ventures. Musical artists like Akon, Lil John, David Banner, 50 Cent, and Jay Z have all undertaken projects to assist in developing infrastructure on the continent of Africa. As pop culture continues to have a strong influence on younger generations, it is helpful to allow it to play a role in the recruitment efforts of Black students. Being knowledgeable of who in pop culture has international reach creates common ground or talking points when recruiting students of color. The best sales people know that establishing rapport and finding a common interest are very important tactics when working with individuals who are interested in what you are offering.

The marketing and promotion side of the study abroad operation is key. University admissions offices have annual budgets designated for printing promotional materials, visits to college recruitment events, and website maintenance. It is important that Black students see themselves as playing a part in the university's international strategies. Black students need to see their fellow classmates: on study abroad brochures, websites, hosting informational sessions, or even employed as student workers in the international office. It is equally important that study abroad alumni are given a platform to discuss their experiences abroad. Word of mouth is also very cost effective as a form of marketing. Numerous study abroad operations at institutions of higher education have prioritized reentry programs for their study abroad alumni. They make sure that study abroad alumni help with their study abroad fair, predeparture orientation, and classroom presentations. An impressive project that I once saw taking place for study abroad alumni was a photography contest. Study abroad alumni were asked to submit the most dynamic image they captured based on categories (nature, service, history, fun). The photographs were enlarged and placed in an exhibition hall on campus. Students, faculty, and staff were able to visit the exhibit hall over a one-week period and vote for their favorite photograph. The winners of the contest were awarded gift cards to some of the city's most popular restaurants.

## Heritage Programming

During 2015–2016, 75 percent of the US study abroad population self-identified as White. Interestingly, more than 54 percent of study abroad activity took place in Europe. Overall, Europe consistently ranks as the most popular study abroad destination for US students. One could argue that European heritage programming contributes to this trend.

Heritage programming is a study abroad experience that relates to a student's personal history and culture. A research project conducted with Black students who studied abroad in Ghana showed that they selected their host country because they were inspired by a quest to discover their personal history and roots (Landau and Moore, 2001). Additional research (McClure, Szelenyi, Niehaus, Anderson, and Reed, 2010) has shown that Asian/Pacific Islanders and Latino/a students may also view heritage as their first priority when choosing a study abroad destination.

It would be naïve to believe that all Black students want to study abroad in Africa. However, it is also naïve to believe that Black students do not have the desire to study abroad in areas where they have roots. In addition to affordability, another benefit to seeking study abroad opportunities in regions where heritage programs are offered is experiential learning. The opportunities to be involved in service learning projects or internships could be simpler to find on these programs.

Heritage programming for Black students is not as rife in other study abroad programs. Study abroad administrators who have a desire to recruit Black students should make an effort to develop and promote heritage programming in their operation's portfolio. Of course, the development of these programs may not necessarily cause study abroad participation among Black students to skyrocket. However, with prior research that heritage programming has a draw on the Black student population, it will be helpful to pose the opportunity to stimulate interest perhaps increase study abroad propensity.

The data indicate that the majority of US students (62 percent) studied abroad for just eight weeks or less. In all, 35 percent of US students stayed for one semester, and only 3 percent of American students stayed long term for a year (Institute of International Education). Having the proper, more desirable programming place for potential students is an instrumental part of recruiting. Developing short-term, heritage based, affordable programming is a solid foundation in garnering interest and potentially increasing participation rates among Black students.

## Faculty

Faculty can be described as the "life blood" of any university study abroad operations. Researchers have stated that the influence of faculty members may have the biggest impact on a student's decision to study abroad. When broken down to sheer numbers, the amount of time faculty members spend with students (as a result of mandatory contact hours required by accrediting bodies) far outweighs the time spent with study abroad professionals in advising or recruitment sessions. Faculty members have the medium to promote study abroad to their students; thus, it is important that study abroad professionals give faculty the knowledge to aid the promotion.

Frequently, study abroad operations contact faculty early on during the academic semester and ask for a ten- to twenty-minute window where their staff can present on the study abroad opportunities for students. I have found these sorts of presentations to be more effective when a study abroad administrators works in conjunction with the faculty member to make the presentation. As previously noted, academic faculty have a lot of influence when it comes to impacting a student's decision to study abroad. Faculty working in conjunction with study abroad administrators and adding to the presentation by discussing; why global competency is important, how it relates to the student's field of study, and what the faculty member has done or is doing with globalization and internationalization efforts can really be effective in reaching students and stimulating interest.

With short-term study abroad programs leading the field in terms of student participation, this presents an opportunity for faculty. Faculty-led programs are popular within the field of study abroad because of the level of familiarity the programs offer. Generally, students are led abroad by their university's academic faculty, travel abroad with fellow university students, and receive academic credit directly from their home university. This type of familiarity creates a level of comfort with some students and parents that makes faculty-led programs the preferred option for some. Study abroad operations can create opportunities for faculty to lead programs, or urge faculty to develop their own programs in their region of interest.

Recruiting new study abroad faculty can be just as difficult as recruiting students. Some faculty members may be working toward tenure, have familial responsibilities, or are just afraid of the liability that comes along with leading study abroad programs. There are a few recruitment tools that can be introduced to study abroad administrators. Firstly, for faculty who are on nine-month assignments, the opportunity for earning during the three summer months could incentivize some academic faculty. Secondly, though some of the time the tenure and promotion process do not consider leading a study abroad program when making decisions about faculty's upward mobility, the added value to a faculty member's curriculum vitae can help when discussing how faculty are contributing to university's international strategic plan, and in end of year reporting's. In some cases, you have faculty who consider all of the incentives but are still not sold on the idea of leading a study abroad program. An interesting initiative by one of South Carolina's largest universities is to open up opportunities for faculty who have never led study abroad programs to serves as program assistants for the more experienced study abroad faculty leaders. The program assistant will help in developing, coordinating and leading the program. He or she will get firsthand experience on the entire process for start to finish. After this experience, the new faculty member will know what goes into a study abroad program and if it is something they are willing to pursue further.

## The CELTIC Pedagogy

There is a fine line in higher education that lies between faculty and administration. When administrators begin crossing over into the classroom to discuss what is taught and how it's taught, they can be met with a lot of resistance. The same holds true for academic faculty who cross over the administrative line. However, a recent study using multiple universities and data from the 2014 National Survey on Student Engagement (NSSE) shows that certain pedagogical approaches increase the study abroad propensity of college students. The results of the study revealed that gender, race, major, and SES are good predictors of participation in study abroad. Additionally, academic collegiate experiences germane to diversity and societal awareness increased propensity to participate in study abroad.

A pedagogical practice coined the CELTIC approach could lead to a higher study abroad propensity among college students. Faculty members who are able to teach courses in ways that students are able to do the following are able to increase the likelihood of their students studying abroad:

1. Connect learning to societal problems or issues
2. Examine the strengths and weakness of their own views on a topic or issue
3. Learn something that changes the way they understand an issue or concept
4. Try to better understand someone else's views by imagining how an issue looks from his or her perspective
5. Include diverse perspectives (political, religious, racial/ethnic, gender, etc.) in course discussions or assignments
6. Connect ideas from your course to their prior experiences and knowledge

The CELTIC pedagogy opens academic faculty up to a wide array of potential institutional collaborations. Teaching faculty could partner with student-focused offices such as study abroad, orientation, and student organizations. These partnerships could come in the form of attending events for extra credit, and/or co-teaching certain lecture material.

## The Big Payoff

Students and parents are becoming increasingly aware of the financial burden that comes along with the college experience. With student loan debt rises, many people question about whether or not college is worth the price tag. Study abroad can be expensive and a tough barrier for Black students. Parents and students want to hear more about the return on their investment. Articulating the worth of a study abroad experience can be instrumental during the job search. Understanding how and where to place it on a resume, and how to use it as a conversation piece in an interview can help build the confidence and competitiveness of college graduates.

Studies have been conducted which reveal that nearly 90 percent of study abroad alumni secured a job within the first six months of graduation, 50 percent felt that their international experience helped them get their first job, 84 percent felt studying abroad helped them build valuable job skills, and 90 percent got into their first or second choice of graduate or professional school (Tomer, n.d.). Being able to express that study abroad is not just academic tourism, and employers look favorably qualifications such as foreign language skills, cross culture communication, resource management, and adaptability is key in helping convince parents and students that the investment in study abroad could reap solid benefits.

It is an important step for study abroad administrators to assist returnees with learning ways of using their international experience to better position themselves professionally. A practice within the field includes collaborating with university career services offices to learn where to place study abroad experiences on cover letters or resumes. Some programs go as far as holding mock interviews to teach students about way of discussing their international experience and how it better qualifies them for the job position.

## Recommendations

Do not underestimate the impact of the classroom experience. Academic departments within HBCUs should make it a point to emphasize the importance of strengthening global competency in their course offering. Collaborations between international affairs administrators and academic faculty to work on designing a more internationalized curriculum is highly recommended. Adopting a pedagogical approach that increases student's awareness to diversity and social issues, encourages study abroad participation among students and is a progressive step in supporting the mission of HBCUs.

Increase the intrigue. Traveling abroad already comes with its own "prestigious" status. Journeying internationally is now becoming increasingly popular on social media sites. Administrators at HBCUs have to maintain interest in study abroad by allocating resources to promotion, marketing, inviting, popular public speakers, and illustrating how global competency impacts the future of their students.

Advise against the barriers. This chapter detailed the more frequent obstacles that Black students face when attempting to study abroad. Maintaining a positive, can-do approach to study abroad is an integral task when advising Black students. In most of my interactions with students when discussing study abroad, my first and last question is "what's stopping you?" Once students realize that there is usually a rational means of overcoming the barriers to participation, the idea of studying abroad become more of a reality.

Develop strategic relationships. International relationships are important for any study abroad operation. Building strategic relationships to cultivate opportunities for Black students at HBCUs is highly recommended. Study abroad administrators must have a solid understanding of their students and student expectations. Developing relationships with foreign partners that allow for heritage programming and more affordable educational experiences is vital.

## CONCLUSION

International travel is becoming increasingly popular within the Black community. A large amount of international travel is taking place by working class professionals who have the financial means to venture abroad. However, it is imperative to begin providing Black students with opportunities to engage internationally prior to entering the workforce. Becoming globally competent while preparing to enter the labor force is beneficial not only to students and employers, but to the world as a whole.

As HBCUs continue to prepare Black students to be productive members of the workforce, it is necessary to understand the challenges around study abroad participation, how to overcome those challenges, and ardently express the importance of increasing global competency. Demonstrating that importance global competency and influencing participation through discussions surrounding professional progress, employment requirements, alumni testimonials, and even pop culture is a step in the right direction toward creating global citizens.

Moreover, HBCUs continue to serve as nurturing environments for Black students and it is important to recognize the role of the entire academy in supporting study abroad. Study abroad operations need campus wide support from academic advisors, instructional faculty, orientation assistants, career counselors, and others.

Study abroad is an invaluable experience that can be life changing for anyone who takes advantage of the opportunity. The soft and hard skills that can be developed, the growth and maturity that takes place, and the understanding of cultures and customs that were once unknown can help create well-rounded individuals who are ready to be future leaders. The push to increase participation rates among Black students will not only strengthen students, but it will also strengthen HBCUs presence on the global stage.

## BIBLIOGRAPHY

Amos, O. (January 9, 2018). Is it true only 10 percent of Americans have passports? http://www.bbc.com/news/world-us-canada-42586638.

Bureau of Labor Statistics. (2018). *College enrollment and work activity.* https://www.bls.gov/news.release/hsgec.nr0.htm.

Carter, H. M. (1991). Black students and overseas programs: Broadening the base of participation. http://eric.ed.gov/?id=ED340323.

*Global competence & national needs: One million Americans studying abroad.* (2005). Washington, DC: Commission on the Abraham Lincoln Study Abroad Fellowship Program.

Institute of International Education. (2001–2015). International students at all institutions, 2001/02–2014/15. *Open doors report on international educational exchange.* http://www.iie.org/opendoors.

Lambert, R. (1996). *Parsing the concept of global competence, educational exchange and global competence.* New York: Council on International Educational Exchange.

Landau, J., and Moore, D. C. (2001). Towards reconciliation in the motherland: Race, class, nationality, gender, and the complexities of American student presence at the University of Ghana, Legon. *Frontiers: The Interdisciplinary Journal of Study Abroad, 7,* 25–58. http://www.frontiersjournal.com/issues/vol7/.

McClure, K., Szelenyi, K., Niehaus, E., Anderson, A., and Reed, J. (2010). "We just don't have the possibility yet": U.S. Latina/o narratives on study abroad. *Journal of Student Affairs Research and Practice, 47*(3), 367–386.

Norton, I. (September 26, 2008). Changing the face of study abroad. http://chronicle.com/article/Changing-the-Face-of-Study/25788.

Simon, J., and Ainsworth, J. W. (2012). Race and socioeconomic status differences in study abroad participation: The role of habitus, social networks, and cultural capital. *ISRN Education, 2012,* 1–21.

Streitwieser, B. T. (2014). *Internationalisation of higher education and global mobility.* Symposium Books.

Tomer, J. (n.d.). Going (and staying!) abroad. https://www.collegexpress.com/articles-and-advice/student-life/articles/student-activities/going-and-staying-abroad/.

*Chapter 9*

# White Faculty
# at the HBCU

## *The Minority Experience and the Road to Inclusion*

### Dalton Dockery

The experiences of White faculty at historically Black colleges and universities (HBCUs) as well as the implications of their growing presence has scarcely been explored in the literature. In order for HBCUs to continue to thrive and grow, they must understand the importance of having a diverse faculty and staff. Diversity provides emerging ideas and thoughts from various cultures and backgrounds that leads to greater knowledge and understanding within—and for—an institution.

The discussion on the issues, problems, and challenges that White faculty are confronted with at HBCUs is of importance if these institutions are to remain successful in recruiting and retaining White faculty. Significant challenges must be confronted in order to promote a positive relationship between all faculty members of the university. If White faculty challenges and issues are understood, then, HBCUs could work toward a positive solution, which would include the retention of White faculty at HBCUs. The outcome will be a better understanding of diversity and the continuation of strengthening HBCUs in the process. The overall goal is embedded in the idea of total inclusiveness that will empower the continued growth of the large number of African Americans and increasing White faculty and White students that attend these HBCU institutions.

## LITERATURE REVIEW

The manner in which White faculty members cope with their immersion into the Black college community is completely different from that of a White

103

philanthropist who often provided funding for HBCUs in the early years (Hill, 1982). At the peer level in the HBCU setting, White faculty interact with Black faculty, and the two different cultures and ethnicities can experience social friction. Whites and Blacks historically have always been on opposite sides, economically and socially. However, at HBCUs in a professional setting these two groups sometimes struggle to find common ground. Although there have been immense improvements in the social interactions of Whites and Blacks, there continue to be areas of contention.

The first HBCUs were founded prior to the Emancipation Proclamation Act of 1862; the oldest HBCU is Cheyney State University in Pennsylvania founded in 1837. Whites have been major contributors to HBCUs since their inception but mainly served in the role of philanthropists. It is interesting to note that while Blacks were the driving force behind the establishment of some of the earliest Black colleges, many White-dominated religious organizations provided funding that established Black colleges in the south (Davis, 2008). They were keenly aware of the need to educate Blacks based on their religious beliefs and ideologies.

Most of the research pertaining to White faculty at HBCUs is related to the perceptions of students and peers rather than reports from the faculty members. Two studies will be used as examples as it relates to the experiences of White faculty at HBCUs. The first and probably most widely known study was conducted by Warnat (1976). The study examined the Black student and Black faculty perceptions of White faculty. Warnat developed four typologies from his findings in which each White member was assumed to be generally classified. These typologies were the Moron, the Martyr, the Messiah, and the Marginal Man. These typologies were developed from the perceptions of students and peers but not the perceptions of the White faculty directly. The second is a study by Smith and Borgstedt (1985), titled "Factors influencing adjustment of faculty in predominantly Black colleges." This study looked at the perceptions of White faculty from their perspective. The importance of Smith and Borgstedt's study is their acknowledgment of the significance regarding inclusivity of the White faculty individual perceptions as well. Moreover, the existence of any minority population results in the development of tensions and rifts between groups, usually as a result of power and sense of belonging. White faculty at HBCUs continue to struggle in finding their sense of belonging within the institutions that they serve (Davis, 2008).

Despite a long history with HBCUs, the White HBCU faculty experience is not frequently researched or shared. Additionally, there are only a handful of studies available that might shed light on White faculty's perceptions regarding sense of belonging within HBCUs. The National Center for Education Statistics (NCES) records race and ethnicity for all institutions including HBCUs. HBCUs in 2013 had 56 percent of full-time instructional staff who were Black, 25 percent who were White, 2 percent who were Hispanic, and 10 percent who were Asian. Aside from the aforementioned statistics, there is very little scholarly research. However, Dawson-Smith's 2006 dissertation on exploring the experiences of White Faculty at two HBCUs, examined their place at the institutions from a historic perspective. The researcher found that one of the key components of successful White faculty at HBCUs is a thorough "socialization" into the culture of HBCU life. This would help White faculty in adapting and coping with a culture that in most situations would be different from their own which is an integral part of their success.

Some of the greatest challenges that White faculty reported in Dawson-Smith's dissertation related to barriers they encountered with promotion and tenure. These types of barriers should be addressed by HBCUs at the fundamental level if they are to be successful in recruiting and maintaining White Faculty. HBCUs must be proactive in reducing not only these types of challenges but any challenges that might hinder progress in this area.

Morris (2015) found that when speaking with White faculty about their experiences, there was a reoccurring theme—White faulty are just as reluctant to criticize HBCUs as they are to criticize predominately White institutions (PWIs). Even when they do identify a problem, they tend to rationalize it. Arguably, the tendency of White faculty to rationalize or dismiss perceived issues at HBCUs may be an attempt to avoid Warnat's typologies.

The Moron category is a professor who is perceived as incapable of securing a position at a PWI and the HBCU is his/her only alternative. The Martyr professor teaches at an HBCU in an attempt to recompense personal racial guilt and wants to make amends for the injustices of the world. This type does not typically complain about any situation and many times commits to working with the Black community. The Messiah professor feels superior to Blacks and hopes to save them from social, intellectual, and spiritual damnation. The professor generally finds themselves in conflict with their Black faculty peers and fosters a relationship devoid of trust with the student body. The Marginal professor strives for acceptance and attempts to bridge the gap between Blacks and Whites. Many times, these individuals tend to focus on their own agendas in contrast to faculty who support the missions of the HBCUs where they are employed (Warnat, 1976).

In many ways, these simple typologies may reflect some of the White faculty at the more than 100 HBCUs in the United States. Warnat's study does not provide the true voices or prospective from the White faculty point of view. In essence, these typologies do not reflect the voices of White faculty and were based on Black faculty and student observations and interpretations. However, Smith and Borgstedt conducted a study that addressed the experiences and perspectives and attitudes of White professors at HBCUs.

This study may provide a more thorough understanding of the experiences of White faculty because it addresses the White faculty voice.

Smith and Borgstedt (1985) explored the experiences of White faculty at six HBCUs and the researchers focused on the White faculty members' adjustment to their minority status. Smith and Borgstedt revealed that 75 percent of the faculty felt socially accepted by their Black peers and students, while approximately one-third expressed a belief that Black faculty members possessed negative stereotypes about them. The majority of the professors, however, articulated that they were committed to the goals of their respective colleges and were supportive of the college community. Approximately 40 percent reported that their White friends had made disparaging remarks about their employment at an HBCU and that almost a quarter of the White faculty reported family members' assigned shame to their HBCU employment.

The voices of the White faculty from this study provide their prospective on how they are viewed by peers, students, and friends as well as their overall acceptance at HBCUs. The fact that many of the faculty felt socially accepted by their Black peers and students speaks volumes in terms of how HBCUs are racially and ethnically accepting to minority faculty. However, this interpretation does not mean that tensions and rifts do not exist. It just reveals that HBCUs have a tendency to be more inclusive.

Given the literature, the overarching focus is the utilization of this information in terms of helping HBCUs become better at providing an environment that will attract minority audiences and further the relevancy of HBCUs in contributing to education, inclusion, and diversity.

## Improving Minority Representation at HBCUs

Smith and Borgstedt (1985) found that White faculty at HBCUs face a myriad of issues including (a) Black faculty members possessing a negative stereotype, (b) White friends making disparaging remarks about their employment at an HBCU, (c) White faculty family members assigned shame to their employment at an HBCU, and (d) White faculty members at times felt isolated at their HBCU. The key factor in addressing many of these issues centers around open dialogue. Strategic planning and receptivity will assist HBCUs in conducting crucial conversations about race and cultural differences. These conversations need to consist of mutual respect and trust as it relates to White faculty representation on HBCU campuses across the nation. There needs to be assurances from administrators that White faculty will be accepted in a safe, honest, and engaging environment. White faculty need to understand the historical and cultural nature of HBCUs. Both have to be able to express their views and build relationships that will only strengthen the success of the university.

In terms of strategic planning, the intentionality of White faculty recruitment is important. There should be an effort to recruit in areas were White professors and faculty members live, attend faith based organizations, and congregate. For example, professional development organizations that are not specifically geared toward minority groups but cater to the brightest and smartest regardless of status are a great place to start. To be competitive, in terms of diversity, HBCUs should consider developing a keen sense and understanding of White faculty background, motivations, family structures, and academic preparedness. In a sense, the question must be answered, *what would motivate potential White faculty to want to come to and remain at an HBCU?* Moreover, the question can be explored in the broader sense of diversity to the inclusion of racial and ethnic diversity that extends beyond the traditional thoughts of Black and White. Indeed, brain trust can be found among any racial or ethnic group. The notion of the recruitment and retention of the *best and brightest* among faculty could eventually extend beyond solely White faculty. This expanded recruitment and retention of intellectual capital will be integral to the sustainability of the HBCU institutional model.

One of the greatest benefits of attending an HBCU is the inclusiveness and diversity of the student body. Those who attend an HBCU get a far more diverse faculty experience than they do if they attend the average PWI. But it is important to understand that continued success means a greater understanding of not only the HBCU culture but the culture of PWIs as well and how the two can work together for the greater good.

White faculty at HBCUs have developed strategies that help them in coping with being a faculty member, just as Blacks adjust to being in the minority at a PWI. Many White faculty have learned of the historical disparities in funding minority-serving institutions at all levels of education and have become passionate about issues of equity. Additionally, White faculty have begun to understand the privileges that come along with being White. Their experiences at an HBCU allowed them to communicate with their White peers about their experiences more effectively. This also assisted in terms of understanding the true value of HBCUs and their importance in US higher education.

## The Modern HBCU and the *Inclusive* Way Forward

In the twenty-first century HBCUs continue to shine as a beacon for equality and justice. With the consistent efforts to end affirmative action in America, it is important that we recognize more than ever the need for inclusiveness and diversity. However, in light of such great accomplishments by HBCUs there is still an undercurrent of racism that exists. Even in a nation where tolerance is often promoted, we find that injustice still exists socially, financially, and geographically.

As a researcher, I have committed a lot of time to the study of a theory called *social dominance theory* (Aiello, Pierro, and Pratto, 2013). It is applicable in this situation as it relates to the discussion surrounding White faculty at HBCUs. Social dominance is more than just one group or culture having influence over another group. It is a complex theory in terms of how psychologically one group can mentally oppress another group. HBCUs should be especially careful not to unintentionally subscribe to the tenants of social dominance that might exist in a micro-cultural environment on a college campus. If HBCUs fail to recognize social dominance on their campuses in terms of White faculty then equality and respect for diversity will suffer. Social dominance is ingrained not only in the organizational and institutional structures of universities but also in the very fabric of our whole American society. In so much that most majority groups are unable to notice the effects of it even though it is seemingly obvious. In Guthrie's book *Even the Rat Was White* (2003) the social dominance theory was at the core in the development of how our American society developed core beliefs about psychology and the understanding of the inner workings of the human mind. Early in the history of developing countries, the differences between the races was not to show the value in diversity but as a way to set up a hierarchal society in which you would have a dominant race and culture.

As this issue continues to be examined, research studies are significant for both the practitioners and researchers in university administration, in terms of the development of policy that could lead to the retention and advancement of White faculty in leadership positions at HBCUs. One of the greatest things about the previously mentioned studies is that participants had an opportunity to reflect on their roles as faculty at an HBCU. I believe it all comes down to one simple word "Leadership." In the art of Leadership, one must understand and meet the needs of "All" those they lead. The focal point of leadership should be group oriented and never individualistic in terms of "I" rather than "We." Great leaders understand that success is brought about from—and should be attributed to—the group rather than individuals or subgroups and in-groups of individuals.

## Recommendations

As the United States continues to change and the population evolves into a sea of diversity, it is incumbent upon leaders to recognize in the HBCU setting that we are living in a multicultural society and inclusion is vital to the sustainability. Educational leaders must be mindful that when policy is developed, it should be implemented with inclusion and fairness at its core. The minority

Table 9.1    Issues of Non-Inclusiveness and Solutions

| *Issues of Non-Inclusiveness* | *Solutions* |
| --- | --- |
| Policy development | Inclusiveness of fairness, love, and justice for all in the development of policy. |
| Culture | All cultures must be valued equally. |
| Decision-making | Inclusive of all individuals in the decision-making process regardless of ethnicity or race. |
| Frank conversation/honest discourse | Departments and campuses should work with all faculty and strategize how to overcome historical and societal influences that affect Blacks/Whites and women in the academic settings. |

experience at HBCUs is a unique one and is, ideally, referenced with the same value as any other cultural experiences that may exist. Attention to minorities in the decision-making process and the intentional elevation of their voices are integral to the continued success of the HBCU. This may be difficult for some universities to accept because it is not consistent with the universities vision or existing priorities. However, HBCUs should engage in honest discourse about the historical and societal influences that affect both Black and White faculty and staff in the academic settings. This conversation could then translate into a strategy focused on overcoming prevalent obstacles and challenges. Long-term, sustainable solutions are not only possible, but a necessity of insuring the survival of an institution, a way of life, a way of American life (Table 9.1).

## REFERENCES

Aiello, A., Pierro, A., and Pratto, F. (2013). Framing social dominance orientation and power in organizational contest. *Basic and Applied Social Psychology, 5,* 487–495.

Davis, A. L. (2008). Examining White faculty maladjustment at historically Black colleges and universities. *The National Journal of Urban Education & Practice, 2*(3), 130–136.

Davis, A. L. (1979). White teachers at Black colleges: A case study of Morehouse College. *The Western Journal of Black Studies, 3,* 224–227.

Dawson-Smith, K. (2006). *White faculty at historically Black colleges and universities.* University of New Orleans, Thesis and Dissertation, 1–149.

Guthrie, R. (2003). *Even the rat was White.* Boston, MA: Pearson.

Guyden, J. A., Foster, L., and Miller, A. L. (1999). White faculty at historically Black colleges and universities: A historical framework. In L. Foster, J. A. Guyden, and A. L. Miller (Eds.), *Affirmed action: Essays on the academic and social lives of White faculty members at historically Black colleges and universities* (1–13). Lanham, MD: Rowman & Littlefield.

Levy, C. (1967). *The process of integrating White faculty into a predominantly Negro college.* Washington, DC: Department of Health, Education, and Welfare (ERIC Document Reproduction Service No. ED 052 744).

Morris, C. (2015). White faculty deal with the challenges of teaching at HBCUs. *Diverse Issues in Higher Education, 32*(4), 12–13.

News and Views. (1998, Summer). White professors teaching at historically Black colleges. *Journal of Blacks in Higher Education, 20*(3), 62.

Pettigrew, T. F. (1971). The role of Whites in the Black college of the future. *Daedalus, 100*(3), 813–832.

Redinger, M. A. (1999). You just wouldn't understand. In L. Foster, J. A. Guyden, and A. L. Miller (Eds.), *Affirmed action: Essays on the academic and social lives of White faculty members at historically Black colleges and universities* (23–35). Lanham, MD: Rowman & Littlefield.

Slater, R. B. (1993). White professors at Black colleges. *Journal of Blacks in Higher Education, 1*, 67–70.

Smith, S. L. (1982). *Dynamics of interracial relationships involving White faculty in Black colleges: Review, systematization and directives.* Paper presented at the annual meeting of the Council for Social Work Education, New York.

Smith, S. L., and Borgstedt, K. W. (1985). Factors influencing adjustment of White faculty in predominately Black colleges. *Journal of Negro Education, 54*(2), 148–163.

Warnat, W. I. (1976). The role of White faculty on the Black college campus. *Journal of Negro Education, 45*(3), 334–338.

*Chapter 10*

# How HBCUs Benefit from Acknowledging the Connection of Ethics and Faith

## *Influences of the Leadership Styles of Black Women in Higher Education*

### Emetrude Lewis

As women are increasingly entering leadership roles that traditionally have been occupied by men, the possibility that the leadership styles of women and men differ continues to attract attention (Eagly and Johannesen-Schmidt, 2001). Leadership has usually been construed as a masculine endeavor with special challenges and pitfalls for women. The patriarchal model of leadership emphasizes a hierarchical approach in which leaders initiate structure while demonstrating autonomy, strength, self-efficacy, and control. The masculine model of leadership is theorized as representative of male values and is most often associated with men's socialized communication patterns (Parker, 2001).

Women entering leadership positions face barriers and many times give up because they become overwhelmed in dealing with barriers. The spotlights of scrutiny under which women lead induces stress factors that will no doubt cause them to interconnect with their inner beliefs and values. In true ethical dilemma, most women tend to reach into their inner resources. Faith helps women to set their priorities and to live with the consequences of their actions (McCoy, 2001).

Previous studies on women's leadership do not account for how Black women leverage their strengths to lead. The debate about the differences between men and women leadership styles has emerged over the last several decades as more women are becoming leaders in the workforce. As more women came into the workforce, it was important in performance management to study their leadership styles, and provide opportunities for women to develop their leadership in the work world. Carli and Eagly (2001) presented research over the decades highlighting women's disparities in top-level leadership positions, as compared with men's positions. The authors argued the research compiled proves the theory of the "glass ceiling" (631) as a plausible reason for the discrepancy. The authors argued that because the mid-manager positions were filled with women, the "pipeline" (631) should be filled with equally qualified women as men for upper-level management leadership opportunities. Though this was certainly a viable argument for the misrepresentation of women in top-level leadership positions, the review of the literature examined the glass ceiling as the only explanation.

## Women in the Workforce

Women comprise 51 percent of the labor force and provide a significant pool of potential leaders. Women predominate in lower-level managerial ranks and are only marginally represented at the executive levels. The US Bureau of Labor Statistics (2014) reported the following percentages of women in managerial positions by ethnicity: Whites, 39 percent; African Americans, 31 percent; Asians, 46 percent; and Latinas, 22 percent (see figure 10.1). Currently, women comprise only 2.5 percent of senior-level or executive leadership positions. Women accounted for only 14.7 percent of Fortune 500 Board seats in 2005. Of these positions, 79 percent were held by White women, and 21 percent were held by women of color.

Women occupy only 24 (2.4 percent) of the CEO positions in the Fortune 1000. This proportion has remained stable in the past decade although the

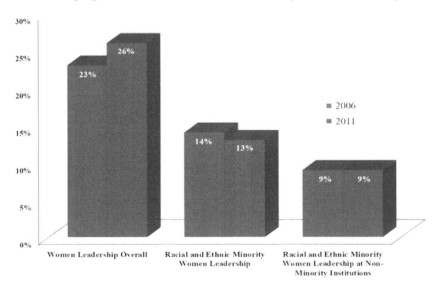

**Figure 10.1    Percentage of women in managerial positions by ethnicity.** *Source:* Adapted from the US Bureau of Labor Statistics 2014 report (www.bls.gov).

situation may slowly be changing (Sanchez-Holes and Davis, 2010). Obviously absent from the current research on women leadership styles are the experiences from Black women who describe how they connect ethics and faith and how these experiences impact their ways of leading. Black women, in general, who work in executive, administrative, and managerial staff positions in institutions of higher education represented only 11 percent (Henry and Glenn, 2009). Current research continues to reveal that issues of racial and gender inequality remain extremely salient features within American higher education, especially for Black women working in higher education (Henry and Glenn, 2009).

In public institutions of higher education, women are underrepresented in senior-level leadership positions compared to their male colleagues (Coleman, 2003; Madden, 2005). A report by the National Center for Education Statistics (NCES, 2012) provides a sobering look at the continuing challenge of diversifying the ranks of the college leadership. While women have increased their representation to 26 percent in 2011, an increase from 23 percent in 2006, the proportion of women leaders who are racial and ethnic minorities declined slightly, from 14 percent in 2006 to 13 percent in 2011. However, when minority-serving institutions are excluded, only 9 percent of women leaders belong to racial or ethnic minority groups, unchanged from 2006.

## Womanist Theory

Critical race theory hypothesizes that race and racism are the main principles in understanding the ways in which theory, policy, and practice are used to lesser African American people, while upholding White supremacy in the United States (Solorzano, 1997; 1998). Gaetane, Williams, and Sherman (2009) utilized critical race theory in their study to explain the experiences of African American women leaders in higher education and examine the intersectionality of race and gender. Black women's Afrocentric ways of knowing emerges from the richness of their African roots, which inform what they believe to be true about themselves and their experiences. Black women draw from common experiences that historically connect them to the fundamental elements of an Afrocentric epistemology (i.e., oppression resulting from colonialism, slavery, apartheid, imperialism, and other systems of racial domination) (Collins, 2000; McLean and Johansen, 2006).

The term "womanism" was developed in response to the dissonance between the gendered focus of the Westernized feminist movement and the cultural experiences of racial and ethnic minorities. It is a feminist ideology meant to situate gender within the major contextual implications of race and class (Hudson-Weems, 2001). Like other critical theorists and social justice activists, womanism views gross differentials in power and resources as highly problematic because they contribute to dehumanization and interfere with individual and collective well-being (Phillips, 2006).

Like feminism, womanism takes diverse forms. Womanism or "woman-of-color feminism," was first defined by African American poetess Alice Walker (1983), emphasizing "the importance of women's intellectual, physical, emotional, and spiritual wholeness, and stressing the need to create a global community where all members of society are encouraged to survive and survive whole" (Davis, 2004, 33). Walker's treatment of feminist ideology incorporates perspectives of race, gender, and class. Hudson-Weems (1995) also offered a version of womanism, seeking to bridge the racial and class void left by feminism, and the gender void left by Afrocentrism, Africana womanism prioritizes race, class, and then gender (Hudson-Weems, 1997).

Researchers and authors have defined "leadership" in many ways. As leadership research and theory moved away from assumptions that individuals either are or are not a born leader, more researchers and practitioners illustrated new leadership models illustrating leadership was both relational and a process. The word "leader" is found in the English language starting around the year 1300 (Wright, 2005). However, scholarly research on leadership did not begin until the twentieth century. Leadership has been defined in many ways along with multiple conceptualizations. Stogdill (1974) concluded that there were as many different definitions of leadership as there are people who have tried to define it. Burns (1978) stated that a study of the leadership literature revealed 130 definitions for leadership.

Literature suggests that although masculinity is associated with leadership, women possess many strengths and qualities that make them effective leaders. The understanding of gender roles is important in leadership research (Adams and Yoder, 1985). Scholars Eagly and Johannesen-Schmidt (2007) conducted several studies since the 1950s to assess the leadership styles of male and female leaders and the meta-analysis of much of this research found that women and men differ in leadership approaches. Research confirms that female leadership styles have had positive outcomes for organizations with respect to communications, negotiations, structure, and authority. Unfortunately, despite the need for the leadership styles often demonstrated by women, organizations too often expect leaders to be dominant, assertive men.

Despite the sluggish changes made after desegregation, Black women have made many gains in higher education since entering in those revered halls. Nonetheless, many factors such as stereotyping, curricular issues, the climate of the environment, the need for a supportive peer culture, the need for mentorship and role models, among others, still function as obstacles to full development within many institutions (Collins, 2001).

Black women have been participating in American higher education for more than a century and have certainly made great strides toward occupying their rightful place within academia, however, they continue to face myriad personal and professional challenges (Henry and Glenn, 2009). Most studies indicate that most women in academic leadership positions, especially women of color, have experienced exclusion, condescension, isolation, dismissal, communication challenges, lack of validation or appreciation, and failure to receive due credit (Mainah and Perkins, 2015). The place of Black women in higher education has broadened to include the highest-ranking position of a university—the presidency. However, ascending to the presidency is fraught with challenges that seek to limit the power and authority of female presidents (Jean-Marie, Williams, and Sherman, 2009). When employed in these positions Black women find that they must interrogate and challenge biases and stereotypes (Agyepong, 2011).

## Findings and Recommendations

Conceivably, the most distinctive finding of this study was the way these women use their ethics and faith connection in their role as an action of their leadership. All the participants use prayer as an interior action prior to making decisions, or in difficult situations, accepting prayers from others, and pray for their own circumstances.

The prayers of these women were neither considered evangelizing actions, nor were the prayers passive, interior-only attitudes. The participants undoubtedly believed that prayer changes things and directs their leadership. They believed that the Lord answered prayers, and they expressed a strong sense of confidence in the way they lead when prayers were incorporated.

Examining the interconnectedness between ethics, faith, and leadership provides a valuable insight into leader rationale, motivation, retention, ethics, and performance. Multiple studies, including this study, show leaders' demonstration of spiritual values such as fairness, integrity, honesty, humility, respect, and truth found to be clearly related to leadership success. These qualities have been selected because they are prominent in leadership research, but this list is by no means exhaustive. For instance, in creating a model of effective leadership, theorists often include the dimensions of hope, faith, and confidence, which also could be studied as spiritual qualities in relation to measures of leader effectiveness.

Several other spiritual values such as compassion and gratitude have also been generally emphasized in the areas of workplace spirituality, religion, character and ethics education, and positive psychology (Fry, 2005). These qualities have been studied as exhibited in the practices of expressing caring and concern, listening responsively, and appreciating the contributions of others, because these behaviors incline to be more objectively quantifiable and measurable. Similarly, it is easier to examine how often a person engages in reflective practice than to measure an amorphous quality such as a person's faith.

Since most of the spiritual qualities and practices presented here have been commonly recognized as important and positive leader traits and behaviors, further exploration of the relationship between ethics, spirituality, and leadership can provide us with a catalyst for developing a leadership theory that integrates character and behavior, motivation, and performance, in a cross-cultural model. For further development, more empirical research on the effect of the connection of ethics and faith on the leader's own motivation is necessary. A more comprehensive empirical approach is needed such as that used in the many studies surveying effects on followers.

A great deal of empirical research has been done on the effects of reflective practice on the leader as an individual, but aside from the most general effects on group performance, there is little information on effects on followers. The area of research into integrating ethics, faith, and leadership is just beginning to emerge, so much of the knowledge that has been gained has been scattered in different streams located in the fields of business, psychology, communication, human resources, religious studies, and medicine (Reave, 2005). Further data gathering, analysis, and consolidation of the findings in these diverse fields will provide a broad empirical base upon which to build theory and explore interdisciplinary approaches.

Reave (2005) indicates that the spiritual values of integrity, honesty, and humility, and the spiritual practices of treating others with respect and fairness, expressing caring and concern, listening responsively, appreciating others, and taking time for personal reflection have all been linked to quantifiable positive effects for organizations and individuals. They cause leaders to be judged as more effective by both their peers and their subordinates, and they lead to enhanced performance. They have been proven to be associated with increased worker satisfaction and motivation, greater productivity, greater sustainability, and enhanced corporation reputation, which in turn have all been linked to increases in the bottom line of profits (Reave, 2005).

Lafreniere and Longman (2008) presented a study of women from Christian universities, developing workshops and retreats to support women's leadership. The same types of workshops and mentoring relationships should be developed for women leaders from public institutions of higher education. Even current workshops and institutes for women leaders in higher education, like the Alice Manicur Symposium from the National Association of Student

Personnel Administrators, could be informed of how and why women who have connected their ethics and faith employ that connection to their leadership in the field of higher education. These steps can only strengthen current curriculums, awaken latent motivation in others, and encourage women to continue their leadership in higher education.

There is the need to conduct a similar qualitative study, with other women leaders outside of the realm of the institution of higher education, to have a comparative view of women leaders' ethics and faith connection. Do these women also experience a connection between their ethics and faith and do they use that connection to influence their leadership? Additionally, empirical studies need to be constructed to examine Black women leaders in the institution of higher education who do not particularly have an ethics and faith connection and therefore do not have that influence on their leadership.

The findings of this study provide the beginning of a research pathway to study ethics, faith, and leadership connection with professionals in higher education, particularly those who work in public institutions of higher education. Studying the ethic, faith, and leadership connection provides understanding of leadership complexity, most particularly for Black women.

This study illuminates how and why Black women leaders in public institutions of higher education, especially those in HBCUs, connect ethics, faith, and leadership. The findings suggest that faith is at the core of their leadership identity. This finding provides practical approaches in supporting women in leadership development and promotion.

Based on this study and other scholars' perspectives, it is critical that the institution of public education system works to intentionally foster interconnectedness in leaders and educator to help them better appreciate the importance of harmonious coexistence, explore the meaning and purpose in life, and cultivate infinite potential in each person. Yasuno (2008) suggests that if we can nurture future leaders and citizens who embrace a spiritual existence—we can ultimately change the destiny of all humankind.

The intersection of race and gender enlists Black women in a distinctive position to be incessantly misunderstood and stereotyped by others who are not torn by the lines of bias that currently divide White from nonwhite in our society, and male from female (Carter, Pearson, and Shavlik, 1996, 460). The area of research into integrating ethics, faith, and leadership is just beginning to emerge, so much of the knowledge that has been gained has been scattered in different streams located in the fields of business, psychology, communication, human resources, religious studies, and medicine (Reave, 2005). Further data gathering, analysis, and consolidation of the findings in these diverse fields will provide a broad empirical base upon which to build theory and explore interdisciplinary approaches.

## Recommendations

Miller (1999) stated that there are many layers of wholeness and meaning of which human beings are compiled. In further reviewing the meaning of wholeness, Glazer (1999) described it as the inherent, seamless, interdependent quality of the world in which everything is already connected, in relationship, and in union. If this is so, then leaders and educators in the realm of HBCUs have the task to lead their followers and students to discern this wholeness. The matter of relationship is fundamental in the concepts of wholeness and holistic education. This process is to make room for all relationships and all layers of relationship of the subject to coexist. Flake (1993) included in his holism recognition that faith is the formative force underlying reality.

The important aspect of the connection of ethics and faith to leadership is the motive and driving force for leaders and learners in the institutions of higher education. This connection refers to a transcendence and compassion both in the space of leadership and the classroom that acknowledges the interconnectedness of higher education leaders to follower and educators to learners. Tisdell (2003) implied that an organic baker's bun is made with the purest ingredients from the shelves. In the same way, having that connection of ethics and faith can increase consciousness, stimulate awareness, foster creativity imagination, connect with grander issues of purpose and meaning, and enable connection with that which animates us. Such divine process begins with the willingness of leaders in HBCUs to make that connection of their ethics to their faith as they lead and educate in the arena of academia.

The connection of ethics and faith empower the moral imperative agenda of leadership and learning. The moral connection is a strategy for leaders in HBCUs to holistically lead and educate in academia. Integrating faith and ethics into leading and learning will encourage reflection and introspection as a key strategy for effective leadership and learning. Leaders, administrators, and educators with the ability to connect their ethics to their faith will not only improve the day-today functions of HBCUs but will raise productivity, increase learning and decrease preconceived notions of leadership and education at HBCUs.

## BIBLIOGRAPHY

Adams, D., and Csiernik, R. (2002). Seeking the lost spirit: Understanding spirituality and restoring it in the workplace. *Employee Assistance Quarterly, 4,* 31–44.

Adams, J., and Yoder, J. (1985). *Effective leadership for women and men.* Norwood, NJ: Ablex.

Agyepong, R. (2011). Spirituality and the empowerment of Black women in the academy. *Canadian Women Studies, 29,* 176–214.

Burns, J. M. (1978). *Leadership.* New York: Harper Torch Books.

Carli, L. L., and Eagly, A. H. (2001). Gender, hierarchy, and leadership: An introduction. *Journal of Social Issues, 57*(4), 629–636.

Carter, D., Pearson, C., and Shavlik, D. (1996). Double jeopardy: Women of color in higher education. In C. Turner, M. Garcia, A. Nora, and L. Rendon (Eds.), *ASHE reader: Racial and ethnic diversity in higher education* (460–484). Needham Heights, MA: Simon & Schuster Custom Publishing.

Christo-Baker, E. A., Roberts, C., and Rogalin, C. L. (2012). Spirituality as a vehicle for passing through the stained glass ceiling: Perspectives on African American women's leadership in US organization. *The Journal of Pan African Studies, 5,* 2.

Coleman, M. (2003). Gender and the orthodoxies of leadership. *School Leadership and Management, 23*(3), 325–339. http://dx.doi.org/10.1080/1363243032000112810.

Collins, A. C. (2001). Black women in the academy: A historical overview. In R. O. Mabokela and A. L. Green (Eds.), *Sisters of the academy: Emergent Black women scholars in higher education* (29–42). Sterling, VA: Stylus.

Collins, P. H. (2000). *Black feminist thought: Knowledge, consciousness, and the politics of empowerment* (2nd ed.). New York: Routledge.

Davis, A. J. (2004). To build a nation: Black women writers, Black nationalism, and violent reduction of wholeness. *Frontiers: A Journal of Women's Studies, 25*(3), 24–53.

Dehler, G., and Welsh, A. (1994). Spirituality and organizational transformation: Implications for new management paradigm. *Journal of Managerial Psychology, 9,* 17–26. doi:10.1108/02683949410070179.

Eagly, A. H., and Johannesen-Schmidt, M. (2007). Leadership styles matters: The small, but important style differences between male and female leaders. In D. Bilimoria and S. K. Piderit (Eds.), *Handbook on women business and management* (279–303). Northampton, MA: Edward Elgar.

Eagly, A. H., Johannesen-Schmidt, M. C., and van Engen, M. (2003). Transformational, transactional, and laissez-faire leadership styles: A meta-analysis comparing women and men. *Psychological Bulletin, 129,* 569–591. doi:10.1037/0033-2909.129.4.569.

Eagly, A. H., and Johannesen-Schmidt, M. C. (2001). The leadership styles of women and men. *Journal of Social Issues, 57*(4), 781–797. doi:10.1111/0022-4537.00241.

Flake, C. L. (Ed.). (1993). *Holistic education: Principles, perspectives and practices.* Brandon, VT: Holistic Education Press.

Fry, L. W. (2005). Toward a theory of ethical and spiritual well-being, and corporate social responsibility through spiritual leadership. In R. A. Giacolone, C. L. Jurkiewicz, and C. Dunne (Eds.), *Positive psychology in business ethics and corporate responsibility* (47–84). Greenwich, CT: Information Age Publishing.

Glazer, S. (Ed.). (1999). *The heart of learning: Spirituality in education.* New York: Tarcher/Putnam.

Henry, W. J., and Glenn (West), N. M. (2009). Black women employed in the ivory tower: Connecting for success. *Advancing Women in Leadership Journal, 27*(2), 1–18. http://www.advancingwomen.com/awl/May2009/Copy_AWL _henry_new.pdf.

Hudson-Weems, C. (1997). Africana womanism and the critical need for African theory and thought. *The Western Journal of Black Studies, 21*(2), 79–84.

Hudson-Weems, C. (1995). *Africana Womanism: Reclaiming ourselves* (3rd ed.). Troy, MI: Bedford Publishers.

Jean-Marie, G., Williams, V. A., and Sherman, S. L. (2009). Black women's leadership experiences examining the intersectionality of race and gender. *Advances in Developing Human Resources, 11,* 562–581.

Johansen, P., and Mclean, G. (2006). Worldviews of adult learning in the workplace: Acore concept in human resource development. *Advances in Developing Human Resources, 8,* 321–328.

Lafreniere, S. L., and Longman, K. A. (2008). Gendered realities and women's leadership development: Participant voices from faith-based higher education. *Christian Higher Education, 7*(5), 388–404. http://eric.ed.gov/?id=EJ814225.

Lewis, J. S., and Geroy, G. D. (2000). Employee spirituality in the workplace: A cross-cultural view for the management of spiritual employees. *Journal of Management Education, 24*(5), 682–694.

Love, P., and Talbot, D. (1999). Defining spiritual development: A missing consideration for student affairs. *NASPA Journal, 37*(1), 361–375.

Mainah, F., and Perkins, V. (2015). Challenges facing female leaders of color in U.S. higher education. *International Journal of African Development, 2,* 2.

McCoy, B. H. (2001). Business faith ethics: Making the connection. *Real Estate Issues, 26,* 54.

Miller, R. (1999). Holistic education for an emerging culture. In S. Glazer (Ed.), *The heart of learning: Spirituality in education* (189–201). New York: Tarcher/Putnam.

Neiman, A. (1998). Tales from the front: Reflections of a catholic university administrator on spirituality and leadership. *Catholic Education: A Journal of Inquiry and Practice, 2*(1), 69–81.

Parker, P. S. (2001). African American women executives leadership communication within dominant-culture organizations: Reconceptualizing notions of collaboration and instrumentality. *Management Communication Quarterly, 15,* 42–82.

Phillips, L. (2006). *The Womanis readert.* New York: Taylor and Francis Group, LLC.

Reave, L. (2005). Spiritual values and practices related to leadership effectiveness. *The Leadership Quarterly, 16,* 655–687.

Rosener, J. B. (1990). *Ways women lead.* Harvard Business Review.

Sanchez-Hucles, J. V., and Davis, D. D. (2010). Women and women of color in leadership. *American Psychology Association, 65,* 171–181.

Solórzano, D. (1998). Critical race theory, racial and gender microaggressions, and the experiences of Chicana and Chicano scholars. *International Journal of Qualitative Studies in Education, 11,* 121–136.

Solórzano, D. (1997). Images and words that wound: Critical race theory, racial stereotyping, and teacher education. *Teacher Education Quarterly, 24,* 5–19.

Stogdill, R. M. (1974). *Handbook of leadership: A survey of the literature.* New York: Free Press.

Taneja, S., Pryor, M. G., and Oyler, J. (2012). Empowerment and gender equality: The retention and promotion of women in the workforce. *Journal of Business Diversity, 12,* 43–53.

Tisdell, E. J. (2003). *Exploring spirituality and culture in adult and higher education.* San Francisco: Jossey-Bass.

Tisdell, E. (2001). Spirituality in adult and higher education. *ERIC Digest.* http://www.ericacve.org/pubs.asp.

US Bureau of Labor Statistics. (2014). *The employment situation 2014.* http://www.bls.gov/news.release/pdf/empsit.pdf.

Walker, A. (1983). *In search of our mother's gardens: Womanist prose.* New York: Harcourt Brace Jovanovich.

Wright, M. W. (2005). *Leadership behaviors and practices among leaders of the Churches of Christ.* Unpublished dissertation, Graduate School of Education and Psychology, Pepperdine University.

Yasuno, M. (2008). The role of spirituality in leadership for social change. *Spirituality in Higher Education, 4,* 179–204.

Young, P. (2004). Leadership and gender in higher education: A case study. *Journal of Further and Higher Education, 28*(1), 95–106.

# Index

# About the Contributors

**Dalton Dockery**, PhD, is a native of Nakina, North Carolina. He earned a BS in agricultural education, an MA in agricultural and extension education from North Carolina State University, and a PhD in leadership studies from North Carolina Agricultural & Technical State College. His dissertation and the articles he has published continue to focus on the experiences of minorities in predominately White institutions of higher learning. Dockery is currently the county extension director with the North Carolina Cooperative Extension Service.

Dockery is married to his lovely wife, Sheila Applewhite Dockery, and they have two children, Whitley and Bryson.

**Amber Fallucca**, PhD, serves as the associate director of *USC Connect*, the current quality enhancement plan (QEP) focused on integrative learning at the University of South Carolina. She manages the assessment responsibilities aligned with the QEP and holds an adjunct teaching role in USC's College of Education. She teaches a course focused on intercollegiate athletics and higher education and a course on institutional assessment in higher education. Fallucca also serves on the leadership team for the Student-Athlete Knowledge Community (SAKC) for National Association of Student Personnel Administrators (NASPA). Her dissertation research focused on faculty senator perceptions of intercollegiate athletics, a study funded by the National Collegiate Athletics Association (NCAA).

**Jesse Ford**, ABD, is a graduate research assistant and a higher education PhD student at Florida State University. In this role, he examines the sociocultural contexts that influence the graduate education and professional experiences of underrepresented populations in academia and assists with the coordination of the Black Men and Black Women Research BootCamp. Prior to serving in this role, he served as an assistant director of multicultural student affairs at the University of Miami, where he developed the College MENtality Program, a program design to assist in the matriculation and retention of Black males undergraduate students and provided diversity, cultural, and social justice programing for students.

He completed an MA in higher education and student affairs from the University of South Carolina and a BA in history from Coastal Carolina University.

**LaShanda Y. Hague**, PhD, is a native of Winston Salem, NC. Hague attended North Carolina Agricultural & Technical State University where she received a BA in sociology with a minor in psychology, an MS in adult education with a concentration in higher education and community college leadership and a PhD in leadership studies. In spring 2017, she began teaching higher education courses in the Department of Leadership Studies and Adult Education at North Carolina Agricultural & Technical State University. In her free time, she passionately volunteers with the Strengthen, Care, Atone, Restore the Heart (SCAR) Foundation. The foundation is a nonprofit organization created to establish commitment to excellence in helping women of every cultural, economic, and social background. In 2012, she was appointed as North Carolina State coordinator for the foundation, a position responsible for planning and coordinating events, professional development, and statewide training.

**Emetrude Lewis**, PhD, obtained a PhD in leadership studies from North Carolina Agricultural and Technical State University. She currently serves as an adjunct professor at her alma mater, North Carolina Agricultural Technical State University. Lewis is an active member of Phi Kappa Phi Honor Society where she serves as an officer for the North Carolina A&T Chapter. Lewis serves on several universities and North Carolina statewide committees.

Lewis is devoted to the research side of her graduate training. She has authored and coauthored several articles for journal publications. In the past two years, she presented papers at regional conferences such as the American Educational Research Association (AERA), Association for the Advancement of Education Research (AAER), Women in Educational Leadership Symposium (WIELS), and Rethinking Leadership: Exploring Ethics and Politics in a Global Arena (CITI).

**Terrance M. McAdoo**, PhD, is currently an instructor in the College of Education at the University of South Carolina, and a leadership consultant with McAdoo Consulting, LLC. He began his professional work experience as a transportation consultant for the North Carolina Department of

Transportation, before transitioning into the field of education. As an educator, McAdoo has worked as a teacher assistant (working with autistic children), a professional licensed business teacher (high school), a student affairs counselor, a retention and praxis coordinator, and collegiate instructor.

McAdoo's areas of research interest include social justice pedagogy, conscious hip-hop music, critical race theory, diversity, ethics and leadership, sports ethics and leadership, and African American and African diaspora. More specifically, his research has explored the potential influence of conscious hip-hop music on social injustice awareness of youth within American society. Additionally, McAdoo has published in the *Journal of Urban Education: Focus Enrichment* with regard to "the Minister and Education." He is currently working to complete an autobiographical book, *From the Hood to Hooded*, and a book on relationships concurrently.

McAdoo, who holds two undergraduate degrees (marketing and transportation/logistics), an MA in management, and a PhD in leadership studies, credits much of his success to his father who instilled respect, integrity, and a strong work ethic in him at an early age.

**Maquisha Ford Mullins**, PhD, is the co-founder and CEO of Science & Math Innovators, Inc., a science education and leadership development nonprofit for primary and secondary school students. Mullins also serves as an adjunct faculty member in communications. She received her undergraduate and doctoral education from HBCUs Oakwood University and North Carolina A&T State University respectively. Her MS in advertising from the S.I. New House School of Public Communications guided her to work in both the business and nonprofit arenas in marketing departments, community relations, and small business consulting. She is a member of the International Leadership Association.

**Comfort O. Okpala**, EdD, is a professor and chair for the Department of Leadership Studies and Adult Education, College of Education at North Carolina A&T State University. She is a recognized scholar and her research agenda is grounded in leadership studies, policy, finance, social justice, and resource equity. Okpala has a variety of publications in leading refereed journals such as the *Journal of Early Childhood Education, Journal of Education Finance, Journal of Educational Researcher, Urban Education, Journal of Applied Business, Journal of Negro Education, Journal of College Teaching and Learning, Contemporary Issues in Education Research, Education, Journal of Research Initiative,* and *Instructional Psychology*. Okpala's published articles have received over 700 citations by national and international scholars according to Google Scholar. She is also a noted coeditor of a book series and has authored several book chapters. Okpala has received numerous leadership awards and commendations.

**William Pruitt III**, PhD, currently works as the assistant director of global collaborations with the University of South Carolina's study abroad office. As a strong advocate for increasing international opportunities for underrepresented minorities, Pruitt has established scholarship initiatives and study abroad heritage programs for collegiate students of color. Prior to arriving at the University of South Carolina in 2016, Pruitt worked with Virginia Tech's study abroad operation for seven years in various roles, including the assistant director of student services. As an assistant director Pruitt managed the office's advising process, scholarship portfolio, and predeparture orientation.

In 2007, Pruitt worked at Shanghai Finance University in Shanghai, China as an ESL instructor, and also assisted with the recruitment of foreign faculty for the English language program. Today, Pruitt serves on the subcommittee for the NAFSA: Association for International Educator's Education Abroad Knowledge Community on Diversity and Inclusion in Education Abroad, and as a Fulbright specialist.

He holds a PhD in higher education administration from Virginia Tech, an MA in business administration from Winthrop University, and a BA in political science from Winthrop University.

**Rosline Sumpter**, ABD, is the curriculum and research coordinator at the South Carolina Technical College System. In this role, she completes curriculum approvals for the sixteen technical/community colleges in the state and compiles annual reports on dual enrollment, graduate placement, and program productivity. Rosline is also a doctoral student in the educational administration—higher education program at the University of South Carolina. Her research interests include community colleges, measures of student success, and the intersection of gender and race/ethnicity.

Sumpter earned a BS in chemistry and an MEd in higher education and student affairs, both from the University of South Carolina.

**Kimberly Y. Walker**, PhD, is currently the academic program assessment manager at the USC School of Medicine Greenville where she collects the curriculum and student-related data for aggregation, analysis, and dissemination via reports and presentations. She received her PhD in leadership studies from North Carolina A&T State University, an MEd from Columbia College, and her BA in psychology from the University of South Carolina. Walker resides in Greenville, South Carolina, with her husband, Matthew, and their two children—Mackenzie and Levi. In her spare time she likes to do research on academic assessment planning, read books, and listen to NPR.